BIBLICAL
MINISTRIES
THROUGH WOMEN

JACK W. HAYFORD
Executive Editor

WITH M. WENDY PARRISH

THOMAS NELSON
Since 1798

NASHVILLE   DALLAS   MEXICO CITY   RIO DE JANEIRO

Published in Nashville, Tennessee, by Thomas Nelson. Thomas Nelson is a registered trademark of Thomas Nelson, Inc.

Thomas Nelson, Inc., titles may be purchased in bulk for educational, business, fund-raising, or sales promotional use. For information, please e-mail SpecialMarkets@ThomasNelson.com.

ISBN: 978-1-4185-4925-1

Printed in the United States of America

HB 02.12.2024

TABLE OF CONTENTS

PREFACE

What is a woman's role in the kingdom of God?

An inescapably blessed fact fills the Scriptures: God has ordained that every believer realize the significance of their mission and ministry as His servant. Gender is no restriction intended to limit significance or breadth of dimension in living for or serving Christ: "I will pour out My Spirit upon your sons and daughters . . . upon your menservants and your maidservants" (Acts 2:17, 18).

Jesus lived and taught human dignity at every dimension God intended. This shows in His treatment of both genders. Women accompanied Him and His disciples on their journeys (Luke 8:1–3). He refused a social taboo and talked with the Samaritan woman at Jacob's Well, leading her to a conversion experience (John 4). Jesus allowed Mary to sit at His feet, assuming the role of a disciple (Luke 10:38–42).

Throughout the ages, God has placed His women in positions of service in nearly all levels of authority. Paul's words in Ephesians 2:10 are true for all who love and serve the Lord: "For we are His workmanship, created in Christ Jesus for good works, which God prepared beforehand that we should walk in them." God has a purpose and plan for all His women!

Keys of the Kingdom

KEYS CAN BE SYMBOLS of possession, of the right and ability to acquire, clarify, open or ignite. Keys can be concepts that unleash mind-boggling possibilities. Keys clear the way to a possibility otherwise obstructed!

Jesus spoke of keys: "And I will give you the keys of the kingdom of heaven, and whatever you bind on earth will be bound in heaven, and whatever you loose on earth will be loosed in heaven" (Matthew 16:19).

While Jesus did not define the "keys" He has given, it is clear that He did confer specific tools upon His church which grant us access to a realm of spiritual "partnership" with Him. The "keys" are concepts or biblical themes, traceable throughout Scripture, which are verifiably dynamic when applied with solid faith under the lordship of Jesus Christ. The "partnership" is the essential feature of this enabling grace, allowing believers to receive Christ's promise of "kingdom keys," and to be assured of the Holy Spirit's readiness to actuate their power in the life of the believer.

Faithful students of the Word of God and some of today's most respected Christian leaders have noted some of the primary themes which undergird this spiritual partnership. A concise presentation of many of these primary themes can be found in the Kingdom Dynamics feature of the *New Spirit-Filled Life Bible*. The new *Spirit-Filled Life Study Guide Series*, an outgrowth of this Kingdom Dynamics feature, provides a treasury of more in-depth insights on these central truths. This study series offers challenges and insights designed to enable you to more readily understand and appropriate certain dynamic "Kingdom Keys."

Each study guide has twelve to fourteen lessons, and a number of helpful features have been developed to assist you in your study, each marked by a symbol and heading for easy identification.

Kingdom Key

KINGDOM KEY identifies the foundational Scripture passage for each study session and highlights a basic concept or principle presented in the text, often along with cross-referenced passages.

Kingdom Life

The KINGDOM LIFE feature is designed to give practical understanding and insight. This feature will assist you in comprehending the truths contained in Scripture and applying them to your day-to-day needs, hurts, relationships, concerns, or circumstances.

Word Wealth

The WORD WEALTH feature provides important definitions of key terms.

Behind the Scenes

BEHIND THE SCENES supplies information about cultural beliefs and practices, doctrinal disputes, and various types of background information that will illuminate Bible passages and teachings.

Kingdom Extra

The optional KINGDOM EXTRA feature will guide you to Bible dictionaries, Bible encyclopedias, and other resources that will enable you to gain further insight into a given topic.

Probing the Depths

Finally, PROBING THE DEPTHS will present any controversial issues raised by particular lessons and cite Bible passages and other sources which will assist you in arriving at your own conclusions.

This *Spirit-Filled Life Study Guide* is a comprehensive resource presenting study and life-application questions and exercises with spaces provided to record your answers. These study guides are designed to provide all you need to gain a good, basic understanding of the covered theme and apply biblical counsel to your life. You will need only a heart and mind open to the Holy Spirit, a prayerful attitude, a pencil and a Bible to complete the studies and apply the truths they contain. However, you may want to have a notebook handy if you plan to expand your study to include the optional KINGDOM EXTRA feature.

The Bible study method used in this series employs four basic steps:

1. *Observation:* What does the text say?
2. *Interpretation:* What is the original meaning of the text?
3. *Correlation:* What light can be shed on this text by other Scripture passages?
4. *Application:* How should my life change in response to the Holy Spirit's teaching of this text?

The New King James Version is the translation used wherever Scripture portions are cited in the new *Spirit-Filled Life Study Guide Series.* Using this translation with this series will make your study easier, but it is certainly not imperative, and you will profit through use of any translation you choose.

Through Bible study, you will grow in your essential understanding of the Lord, His kingdom and your place in it; but you need more. Jesus was sent to teach us "all things" (John 14:26; 1 Corinthians 2:13). Rely on the Holy Spirit to guide your study and your application of the Bible's truths. Bathe your study time in prayer as you use this series to learn of Him and His plan for your life. Ask the Spirit of God to illuminate the text, enlighten your mind, humble your will, and comfort your heart. And as you explore the Word of God and find the keys to unlock its riches, may the Holy Spirit fill every fiber of your being with the joy and power God longs to give all His children. Read diligently on. Stay open and submissive to Him. Learn to live your life as the Creator intended. You will not be disappointed. He promises you!

SESSION ONE

Women of Virtue

Proverbs 31:30 Charm is deceitful and beauty is passing, but a woman who fears the LORD, she shall be praised.

This Kingdom Key verse is from a passage of Scripture familiar to most women. It describes a "virtuous woman." This high standard for womanhood originated with one who was herself a virtuous woman, Lemuel's mother. She presents an inspiring goal. The cultural details of her specific tasks are different in our era, but the principles are timeless.

Read through Proverbs 31:10–31 and note how many verbs it contains; this woman seeks, works, rises, provides, perceives, stretches, extends, reaches—in this short passage, more than twenty verbs are used to describe the actions of this industrious woman. No mention is made of her physical traits; her personality is not described. The picture we are given of this paragon of virtue is made up entirely of her character—the way she interacts with the world around her.

At the heart of this short passage, you will find a powerful truth—"a woman who fears the LORD" has available to her all the things that make for a blessed life filled with joy, appreciation, love, and contentment.

Let us begin our journey through the biblical examples of women of virtue and discover how to walk in the abundant life God means for His women to enjoy.

Read Proverbs 9:1–6, 10; James 1:22–25; 2:14–26.

Questions:

What similarities do you see between Proverbs 9:1–6 and Proverbs 31:10–31?

What do you see as the single most important quality of a virtuous woman? (Proverbs 9:10)

From the passages in James, what reason can you find for the industrious nature of the Proverbs 31 woman?

In what ways do you live an active faith? In what ways do you fail?

Word Wealth—*Virtuous*

Virtuous, *chayil* (khah'-yil); Strong's #2428: a force, whether of men, means, or other resources. In other places in Scripture, this word is also translated as valor, strength, power, and substance. A virtuous woman is a force to be reckoned with because she finds her strength in God.

Kingdom Life—*Eternal Significance*

A virtuous woman not only cares physically for her home and loved ones; she is also a watchman over the emotional and spiritual condition of her family (Proverbs 31:27). The Hebrew word translated as "watches" is *tsaphah* (Strong's #6822), which is translated as watchman in other places in Scripture. Taking her position as watchman seriously, the virtuous woman not only cares for her family with serving, ministering hands (Proverbs 31:20), she also serves diligently as a prayer warrior. This is seen in Proverbs 31:13 wherein the Hebrew word *kaph* is translated as "works." *Kaph* carries the connotation of commitment and preparation of an offering. As used here, it symbolizes upturned hands extended in prayer. Confident in the God to whom she prays, the effective woman knows she has eternal significance.

Read Philippians 4:6; James 5:16.

Questions:

Do you pray for your loved ones regularly and fervently?

_____

_____

_____

In what way does praying for your loved ones give more expression to love than the physical acts of caring?

_____

_____

_____

What are some biblical examples of praying women? What can you learn from their prayer lives?

_____

_____

_____

Kingdom Life—*Meet Your Sisters*

God, through His Word, has given us the opportunity to meet for ourselves many women just like us—women who experienced many of the same challenges, joys, and anxieties we do today. This lesson will allow you to glimpse the women you'll meet as you journey through *Biblical Ministries Through Women* as well as a few others whose stories contain great messages for women today.

Throughout the ages, God chose specific women whose stories would be told in the pages of His Word. He chose them for a reason. Each one has a lesson to teach. If we strive to become virtuous, godly women, we would do well to look to our sisters and discover God's truth as it is presented through their lives.

The following questions are designed to help you begin focusing on some of the women of faith you will encounter in this study. Be as honest and transparent with your answers as possible. This is not a test; the point is the discovery of truth.

Read Genesis 12:1–20; 16:1–6; 18:9–12; Exodus 12:1–9; 15:20, 21; Numbers 12:1, 2; Judges 4; Ruth 2; Esther 10:1–19; Luke 1:26–38; Acts 18:1–26; Romans 16:3; 1 Corinthians 16:19; 2 Timothy 18:26; Acts 16:13–15.

Questions:

In what way(s) can you relate to Sarah?

Nothing is too hard for God. Do your reactions to problem situations reflect that truth?

Is it ever appropriate to criticize those God places in authority?

How important are the things a woman says?

Would you be willing to act as courageously as Deborah on a matter of personal conviction?

From where did Ruth draw the strength and courage to face her difficult trial?

What is a kinsman-redeemer, and how does that relate to you today?

What role did faith play in Esther's life?

What was Mary's response to what was required of her?

_____

_____

_____

What is shown about the nature of God through the mothers of Scripture?

_____

_____

_____

Why do you think true hospitality is such a rare and unusual thing today?

_____

_____

_____

What is God's intended purpose for wives?

_____

_____

_____

What about for women in general? How can we serve Him from our "Jerusalem" (Acts 1:8), from the place of our most immediate influence?

_____

_____

_____

Probing the Depths

Read Ephesians 5:22–33.

Submission is a biblical concept that has become the source of controversy and debate within the church. Some women are offended by the mere suggestion that they subjugate their wills to that of anyone—especially their husbands.

The truth is that all believers are called to live in mutual submission to one another. This applies in a unique way to the marriage relationship.

The wife is called to submit to her husband "as to the Lord." The word translated as "submit" is the Greek word *hupotasso* (hoop-ot-as'-so, Strong's #5293). It means to willingly subordinate, to submit to control, to obey, or to yield. It is a military term that conveys the idea of arranging troops under the command of a leader. In non-military use, it is a voluntarily cooperation for the common good. Thus, a wife is called to serve, honor, edify (build up), and obey her husband. Her attitude toward her husband, according to this terminology—"as to the Lord"—is to be one of highest esteem and regard.

In a matching—even more, an initiating way—the husband is called to lay down his life for his wife. He is to sacrifice his own interests in order to enhance hers. His role is to nourish and cherish. In this way, each marriage partner contributes to bringing the other to their full potential.

A marriage lived out in this mutually loving environment mirrors the interactive love that Christ has for His church and His church is called to have toward Him.

Read 1 Peter 3:5, 6.

Questions:

What are your feelings regarding submission within marriage?

Is there a point where submission is wrong?

_____

_____

Given the atmosphere of today's world, is the topic of submission even a relevant issue anymore?

_____

_____

Read Genesis 2:23, 24. In what ways does this passage pertain to submission within marriage?

_____

_____

Record Your Thoughts

This lesson has provided a peek into the lives of just a few of God's daughters. One important thing to keep in mind is that this and the following lessons barely scratch the surface of some very deep and difficult issues. They are not intended to be exhaustive or to be accepted as the final word; but they should stir you, inspire you, convict you, and perhaps even provoke you into further examination and discovery of God's Word.

Allow the following sessions to lead you to the feasting table of God's Word. Once you've tasted of the King's bounty, you'll willingly accept His invitation to return as often as you can.

In your brief review of these biblical women's lives, what concept(s) did you encounter that seems most foreign to you? In what way?

_____

_____

Make a list of the attributes you see in these women's lives that you desire to cultivate in your own.

_____

_____

SESSION TWO

Sarah, Daughter of Faith

 Kingdom Key—*Absolute Assurance*

Hebrews 11:1 Now faith is the substance of things hoped for, the evidence of things not seen.

This well-known verse is often referred to as the definition of faith. However, it is more aptly understood as a description of how faith works. Faith is an established conviction concerning things as yet unseen and a settled expectation of future reward. The Greek word translated as "substance" literally means "a standing under," and was used in the technical sense of a title deed. The root idea is that of standing under the rightful claim to a property to support its validity. Thus, faith is the title deed of "things hoped for." That hope, that assurance, rests on God's promises.

Read 2 Corinthians 1:20.

Questions:

What are the promises you cling to at this point in your life?

_____

_____

In what way should knowing Jesus is the fulfiller and fulfillment of all the promises of God increase your ability to stand firm in your faith?

_____

_____

_____

Kingdom Life—*Triumphant Faith*

In this same chapter of Hebrews, we find Sarah listed as an example of one who, along with her husband Abraham, excelled in faith (11:11). In so doing, she saw God miraculously intervene on her behalf and use her life to further His will. We will examine how her faith endured through many transitions, failures, difficult points of submission, and heartbreaking trials. Though beautiful, Sarah did not rely on her outward appearance (1 Peter 3:3, 4), but displayed great character, grace, dignity, and courage. We can discover much from the life of Sarah that will help us walk in the triumph of faith.

Read Genesis 11:27—23:2.

Questions:

What qualities, positive or negative, do you observe in Sarah?

In what ways can you relate to the various situations in her life?

What about her led to her ability to stand strong in faith in spite of her circumstances?

Probing the Depths

Your study will be enhanced by learning more about Abraham and Sarah. First, you'll notice their original names were Abram, meaning "Exalted Father," and Sarai, meaning "Princess." Turn to Genesis 17:1–22 and read of God's covenant with Abram. It was at this time that God, as a sign of His established covenant, changed Abram's name to Abraham, meaning "Father of a Multitude," and Sarai became Sarah, "The Princess," or "Queen." [NOTE: For ease of reference, they will be referred to throughout this session by their God-given names, Abraham and Sarah.]

If you have further background and cultural questions after this study, they can be answered through study Bibles, reference books, and Bible concordances or encyclopedias. Check with your pastor or a nearby Christian college library for titles and authors. For more about Sarah, you could begin with Ur, the longtime home Abraham and Sarah were asked to leave behind.

Setting the historical stage will increase understanding of people and their actions; knowing more about a time and culture can help prevent misinterpretation or misapplication of Scripture; and being able to get a clear overview can also reveal a pattern of God's dealings.

Kingdom Extra

Though the Bible does not supply much information about Sarah's early years, we do know something of her heritage. Genesis 20:12 tells us that Sarah was actually Abraham's half sister—they shared the same father, Terah. In our society, this type of relationship is considered illegal and immoral; however, familial intermarriage was a common practice during the patriarchal age, especially in tightly knit societies such as the one in which Abraham and Sarah lived.

Bible narrative does not provide many intimate conversations between Abraham and Sarah. But we can learn a bit about their relationship from the facts that are presented. We know Abraham was ten years older than Sarah (Genesis 17:17). We also know Sarah was a beautiful woman who was devoted to her husband (1 Peter 3:5, 6). We can surmise that Abraham and Sarah had a very progressive relationship for the time in which they lived. This is seen in Abraham's willingness to consider Sarah's feelings and listen to her advice and counsel (Genesis 12:5; 16:1, 2, 6). In renaming her, God linked her in corulership with Abraham and included her in His covenant promise. Finally, Genesis 23:2 reveals Abraham's distress at Sarah's death. What little we know of Sarah's marriage tells us she enjoyed a loving, respectful, rewarding relationship with Abraham.

Read Ephesians 5:22; Colossians 3:18.

Questions:

What feelings are provoked by the knowledge that God's Word tells wives to submit to their husbands?

_____

_____

_____

Why do you think you react in this way?

_____

_____

_____

Read Genesis 3. In what way(s) did lack of submission play into this devastating event?

_____

_____

In what ways do you perceive respect (both given and received) affecting the willingness of women to submit?

_____

_____

_____

Probing the Depths

It seems few subjects can ignite the resentment of women faster than that of submission. However, the true nature of submission is not subservience nor does it convey less value on the one called to submit.

In Genesis 3:16, God pronounces judgment upon Eve for the sin she committed. Within that judgment, God said, "Your desire shall be for your husband, and he shall rule over you." Often understood as a statement proclaiming a woman's diminished value, the true meaning is quite drastically different. When God said Adam would "rule over" Eve, He was asserting the divine assignment of the husband's servant-leader role. There is no evidence this was ever intended as a diminishing of a woman's personhood or giftedness; rather, it points to a redemptive role assigned to the husband toward the wife as a means toward reinstating the original partnership. This passage does not assert male dominance over females. It does assign husbandly responsibility for leadership in the marriage relationship (Ephesians 5:22–33).

Kingdom Life—*Embracing the Unknown*

As the story of Sarah begins, she is in the process of moving; it is a time of transition for her—an event that becomes a common one throughout her life. Few of us will ever move so often; however, we will all, in some form or another, face the challenge of leaving a place of familiarity in our lives for some unknown destination, wherein we can only trust the leading of God through the Holy Spirit, or the leading of someone in authority over us.

Sarah was called upon to leave behind her home, Ur. Historians have discovered this thriving, affluent city was a place of culture and commerce. Ur appears to have been a nice place to live, given the standards of the day. Think for a moment about all that Sarah was being asked to forgo in leaving her home, relatives, and familiar associations. Write out what you think her feelings might have been, and why.

Now read Genesis 12:1 and Hebrews 11:8. At this point, Sarah had lost her father-in-law and was still childless at 65 years of age, and God called Abraham to move again; only this time, the destination was unknown.

Read Genesis 12:1–3.

Questions:

Though Abraham most likely shared God's message with Sarah, do you think this move was a challenge to Sarah's faith? Why?

✎ _____

_____

_____

What would be your response if you were given a similar set of circumstances? (Joy, anger, fear, anticipation, dread, hope, anxiety, excitement—choose from these, or add your own.)

✎ _____

_____

_____

What do you believe is the heart attitude that would cause your response?

✎ _____

_____

_____

Kingdom Life—*Empowering Trust*

It appears, given no record of contention or disunity, that Sarah *trusted* Abraham's leading through all these difficult transitions. But it also appears her trust went beyond Abraham. According to 1 Peter 3:5, 6, the basis of Sarah's fearless, submissive spirit was her trust in God.

Remember, Abraham and Sarah did not know *why* they had to leave their home, *where* they were going, *when* they would get there, or *how* God intended to fulfill His promise. They could only trust in *what* they knew about *Whom* they knew!

Although Sarah was imperfect, and, as we'll soon discover, acted rashly on occasion, the Bible never records a single instance of her disobeying her husband. For that, she is praised in 1 Peter 3:6. To aid our understanding, let us examine the words "submissive" and "obeyed," as they relate to this verse in 1 Peter.

We have already examined the meaning of the word "submissive" (see Probing the Depths in Session One). From this definition, we see the model of troops under the command of a leader. A leader is appointed as the one responsible for the welfare and safety of all under his command. Just so, we see a place of protection and freedom for wives as they come under the appointment (or charge) given to a husband by God. As a husband aligns himself with God's order and receives God's appointment to be a covering for his wife (Genesis 3:16; Ephesians 5:23–33), he also comes under God's covering. So in standing under the protective covering of her husband, a wife is also under the larger umbrella of the covering of God. By stepping out from either, she steps out from both.

Word Wealth—*Obeyed*

Obeyed, *hupakouo* (hoop-ak-oo'-oh); Strong's #5219: To hear as a subordinate, listen attentively, obey as a subject, answer and respond, submit without reservation. *Hupakouo* was used particularly of servants who were attentive to the requests made of them and who complied. This word thus contains the ideas of hearing, responding, and obeying.

Kingdom Life—*Wisdom in Submission*

So, even without the benefit of the written Word of God, Sarah understood the wisdom of complying with God's order. (Given their knowledge of God, one wouldn't be surprised if Abraham and Sarah had been recipients of the stories of history, including Adam and Eve and God's command of Genesis 3:16.) She also was clearly not a victim of an insensitive, suppressive master, but was under the canopy of a loving husband who, as we have seen, respected and cared for her.

Read 2 Samuel 22:1–4; Psalm 37:3–5; Proverbs 3:5, 6; 16:20; Jeremiah 17:7, 8; Nahum 1:7.

Questions:

What can you take from Sarah's experience and the scriptures you've studied and apply to your own life when it comes to times of difficult change or transition?

_____

_____

_____

_____

What insight have you gained into the power and safety of submission?

_____

_____

_____

_____

What questions and/or concerns do you have that remain unanswered?

_____

_____

_____

_____

The principle of submission is a challenge to anyone's flesh and grates against the very nature of our human tendencies. It is particularly difficult for women because of the confusion and misapplication of the truth that has existed regarding the subject. But remember that submission is a clear principle established by God out of His all-wise, all-loving omniscience for our protection and blessing. And real freedom, the genuine liberation to be all God intends us to be, can only come through the knowledge of genuine truth (John 8:31, 32), and the application, or living out, of that truth in one's personal life (James 1:22–25). It is in that place of trust in God and His order for our lives that we can walk in the triumph of faith.

It is important to note that this study in no way suggests that a woman should subject herself to harm or abuse in the name of submission; and a husband is charged to not exploit a wife's trust (Ephesians 5:25–29; 1 Peter 3:7). But it is also important to note that a loving wife, with the incorruptible beauty of a gentle and quiet spirit, is precious not only to her husband (Proverbs 31:10, 11), but also in the sight of God (1 Peter 3:4).

Record Your Thoughts

In your own words, write a definition of submission. Be as thorough as you can, keeping in mind the biblical insights of this session.

Think about all those in your life who are in some place of authority over you (a pastor, an employer, the Lord). List as many as come to mind. In light of what God is teaching you about submission, write next to each one the ways you can adjust your relationship in order to better align yourself under their covering. Use a Bible concordance to find a scripture reference to support your "adjustments."

Example:

Person	Adjustment	Bible reference
Husband	Treat him with more respect	Ephesians 5:33
	Trust his leading	1 Peter 3:6

Christ can enable you to fulfill these desires and walk in a manner pleasing to God but you *must* ask of Him what you need. Take time to prayerfully lift this list to God that He might grant you everything necessary to live a released life of submissive, powerful faith.

SESSION THREE

Sarah and
Lessons of Faith

 Kingdom Key—*Instruction in Righteousness*

2 Timothy 3:16–17 All Scripture is given by inspiration of God, and is profitable for doctrine, for reproof, for correction, for instruction in righteousness, that the man of God may be complete, thoroughly equipped for every good work.

There are vital lessons throughout Scripture that teach us the godly response to various trials or circumstances. But also included in God's Word are examples of failure, accompanied by the redemption of God, His judgment, or the natural result of sin. Since *all* of Scripture is inspired by God, and is "profitable for doctrine, for reproof, for correction, for instruction in righteousness," there is evidently as much to learn from the failures of people as from the successes.

Therefore, we will examine several occasions when Sarah and others went beyond godly action through faith and took matters into their own hands. Let us also pay close attention to the consequences of their failure to trust the full promise of God.

Read Proverbs 3:5, 6.

Questions:

What difference do you believe it would make in your life if you began each day with this verse as your guide?

What is the heart attitude at the core of this way of life?

What challenges do you face in attempting to live your life of faith based on this verse?

 Kingdom Life—Refuse Doubt

Sarah's childlessness was devastating to her because bearing children was central to the identity of a Hebrew woman. God Himself had commanded His people to be fruitful and multiply (Genesis 1:28). The agreement to produce an heir was even part of the marriage vows. In ancient Israel, a child was considered part of God's blessing; childlessness was thought to be His curse (Deuteronomy 28:1–4, 15–18).

We have already examined Sarah's faithful response to God's dealings with Abraham and her willingness to follow his leading. Regardless, as the years passed, though they experienced blessing and provision, they remained childless. This was confusing even to Abraham (Genesis 15:2).

Over the next decade, Sarah allowed a seed of doubt to land in the soil of her heart. Granted, all the natural circumstances gave her reason to wonder about God's promises. But she had already experienced God's supernatural intervention on her behalf when He protected her from Pharaoh (Genesis 12:14–20). Yet, Sarah allowed the seed of doubt to remain, and it grew to unbelief. She decided God needed her help and took matters into her own hands. She attempted to produce an heir for Abraham through her maidservant. Although she allowed doubt to cloud her thinking, it was this act, and not the doubt, that was Sarah's first failure. But rather than cry out to God for help, Sarah allowed unbelief to grow; this led her to act according to the flesh, apart from God (Galatians 4:23).

Read Mark 9:14–27; Hebrews 12:1, 2; James 1:6.

Questions:

Have you ever experienced crippling doubt when faced with trials you don't understand?

_____

_____

What has been your reaction in the past when doubt clouds your mind?

_____

_____

_____

According to Mark 9:14–27, what is a more productive and healthy reaction?

_____

_____

What (or Who) is the source of faith?

_____

_____

When you are tossed about by questions and doubt, what steps can be taken to assure doubt and unbelief are overtaken by faith?

✎ _____

_____

_____

Behind the Scenes

In biblical days, slaves or servants held a place as a part of the household. Although they were not considered family members, they were seen as extensions of their masters.

When Abraham complained to God that his heir was "one born in [his] house" (Genesis 15:3), he referred to his slave, Eliezer. Abraham's culture permitted a senior slave to become heir of a childless man. Because Sarah remained barren, Abraham feared his only heir would be one not of his blood.

Female slaves, especially those who served as personal maids to the mistress of the house, were also seen in many ways as an extension of the one they served. Hagar, Sarah's personal maid, was likely a favorite servant in the household as it is believed she was probably a gift from Pharaoh (Genesis 12:16, 20). Ironically, if this is true, she was a symbol of God's provision and protection for Sarah.

It was within Sarah's legal right to give Hagar to Abraham; it was common practice in those days for a childless woman to allow her husband to father children through her maid. This was even often encouraged when a man had no heir to receive his estate. When maids were given over to the master of the house, they became concubines.

Concubines were accepted and commonplace in those times. Many Old Testament figures had concubines, including: Jacob (Genesis 30:4), Gideon (Judges 8:31), Saul (2 Samuel 3:7), David (2 Samuel 5:13; 15:16), and Solomon (1 Kings 11:3).

(To read the laws concerning concubines, see Exodus 21:7–11; Leviticus 19:20–22; and Deuteronomy 21:10–14.)

Kingdom Life—*Reject Pride*

Sarah's plan succeeded and Hagar conceived. But her attitude toward Sarah became haughty and demeaning (Genesis 16:5). She stabbed again and again at a difficult issue for Sarah—her pride. It was pride that led Sarah to cover her embarrassment and provide herself with an heir; and it was likely the same pride, coupled with her own feelings of inadequacy, that caused her to despise Hagar. There is no doubt Sarah regretted her decision to take matters into her own hands.

Pride is insidious. It creeps in when we are weakest and spreads its poison before we are aware. It is pride that causes one to challenge the validity of God's Word (Genesis 3:1–5). Pride causes us to consider our own devices rather than wait for God's hand to direct our lives. And as Sarah learned only too well, prideful things done in the flesh may seem enticing and clever at the time; but the negative results can snowball quickly.

Read Proverbs 8:13–21; 13:10; 16:18; 29:23; 1 John 2:15–17.

Questions:

How is pride contrary to faith?

_____

_____

How is pride contrary to wisdom?

_____

_____

In your view, how are faith and wisdom linked in the heart of a believer?

_____

_____

_____

When in your own life has pride caused you to take matters into your own hands?

What was the outcome?

How might walking in faith and wisdom have changed the outcome?

What steps can you take to guard against choosing pride rather than faith in the future?

Kingdom Life—*Listen and Grow*

Listening to Sarah's voice had originally been folly for Abraham. Her advice set in motion untold difficulty and heartache that would last for centuries. The situation was a sad mirror of Adam's folly in listening to Eve when the world was new.

But as we pick up Sarah's story in Genesis 21, many years have passed since that earlier, fateful day. Sarah has grown and matured; she has learned to listen rather than react. Even her name has been changed. And at this point, God tells Abraham to listen to his wife and send

Hagar and Ishmael away. God clarifies to Abraham that His plan is still in place—His covenant promise would be fulfilled through Isaac, the one given to Sarah and Abraham together.

God has never veered from His original design—man and woman working together to increase His kingdom in the world (Genesis 1:26–28). A woman's effectiveness multiplies when she is confident that she has a powerful place in the ongoing purposes of God. This confidence will grow and mature as she is affirmed by her husband (or male counterparts in the workplace or other relationships).

Read Genesis 2:18—3:24.

Questions:

What similarities can you discover between Eve and Sarah?

What heart attitude led each of these women to go against the will of God?

In what ways do you find these same sinful attitudes infringing on your own walk of faith?

Read Psalm 119:11. How does having the Word of God planted in your heart guard against sin?

How can keeping the Word of God close to your heart help you make decisions in line with God's will?

✎ _____

_____

_____

Behind the Scenes

Eve was divine inspiration in every respect, fashioned in perfect form by the hand of God. God's ultimate gift to Adam was an enticing package, displaying beauty of form and grace in manner. Inwardly was sure to be found intelligence, humor, creativity, inspiration—an eternal gift that could be rediscovered again and again. Her environment was lovely, her relationship exciting, her every need was met, and all unimpaired by sin.

Eve's downfall was not initially a case of blatant rebellion, but began when she doubted God's Word was true. Though she became the first to violate the divine regulations governing their life (2:16, 17; 3:6), the Word of God holds Adam as the disobedient one—the one who knowingly broke trust with God (Romans 5:12, 17; 1 Timothy 2:14). This fact does not intimate that the woman was less intelligent or more vulnerable to deception than the man, but that under the circumstances in which the fall of man occurred, deception of the woman preceded active disobedience of the man. Thus, it is clear that our lack of faith in God's Word can open wide the door to deception.

The same tactic used on Adam and Eve continues to be an often-used weapon in our enemy's arsenal. Rather than tempt us with an obvious ploy that we would surely recognize and deny, he encourages us to speculate about what might be ours if we reach for things contrary to God's desire.

Read Proverbs 1:7; 30:5.

Questions:

What was the basic problem in Eve's desire for wisdom as seen in Genesis 3:6?

In what way do Christians today suffer from the same delusion?

What does God make clear about our changing His Word to suit our own desires?

How would you describe the "fear" that leads to wisdom?

How might this wisdom be obtained?

Word Wealth—*Wisdom*

Wisdom, *chochmah* (choach-mah′); Strong's #2451: Wisdom; skillfulness, whether in the artistic sense (craftsmanship) or the moral sense (skills for living correctly). Biblical wisdom unites God, the Source of all understanding, with daily life, where the principles of right living are put into practice. One is exhorted to make God the starting point in any quest for wisdom (Psalm 111:10). Therefore, seek wisdom above all else in order to live successfully (Proverbs 4:5–9).

Record Your Thoughts

Eve and Sarah suffered immeasurable losses because they doubted God's Word and relied upon their own wisdom (or lack thereof). And both influenced their husbands to participate in their faithless acts, the results of which humankind still bears.

But praise be to God, our Redeemer! It is a remarkable token of divine grace that God, in His mercy and in His giving of the first promise of a Deliverer/Messiah (Genesis 3:15), chose to bring this about by the Seed of the woman. In short, the one first scarred by sin is selected to be the one first promised to become an instrument of God's redemptive working. And Sarah was allowed the immense privilege of participation in the royal genealogy of the Lord Jesus Christ, not by what she earned or deserved, but by His marvelous grace and love.

List the characteristics you find in both Eve and Sarah. As you consider this list, honestly compare your own personality traits to theirs. What areas do you find in which you need to listen and grow? Which areas are prideful? Are you in need of godly wisdom?

_____

_____

_____

_____

In an honest self-appraisal, to one degree or another, we all will discover our need for true, godly wisdom. Read James 1:5 and then peruse the Proverbs. List all the benefits of wisdom and all the advice given to gain those benefits.

✎ _____

_____

_____

_____

Wisdom is available to all God's children. Only ask and believe.

ADDITIONAL OBSERVATIONS

SESSION FOUR

Miriam, Daughter of Ministry

 Kingdom Key—*Equal in Christ*

Galatians 3:26–28 For you are all sons of God through faith in Christ Jesus. For as many of you as were baptized into Christ have put on Christ. There is neither Jew nor Greek, there is neither slave nor free, there is neither male nor female; for you are all one in Christ Jesus.

This verse in Galatians is hard to misunderstand. It clearly states that, in Christ, all are equal. This should not be misconstrued to deny or hinder individuality or the unique qualities and characteristics each of God's children possesses. It should, however, lead us to understand that no one person is of greater intrinsic value than another in the eyes of God. This fact is made clear in Acts 10:34 when Peter says that "God shows no partiality."

Read Joel 2:28; Acts 1:11–14, 2:1–4.

Questions:

Does anything in these verses lead you to believe only men are empowered by God to minister to His people?

_____

_____

_____

What are your beliefs as to a woman's role in church life?

_____

_____

_____

Upon what biblical principle or content do you base your beliefs?

_____

_____

_____

Kingdom Life—*Miriam, Daughter of Influence*

To prepare for this session, read chapter 14 and 15 of Exodus and Numbers 12.

When God called Moses to lead the Hebrews from Egyptian captivity, Moses' brother, Aaron, and his sister, Miriam, shared in the call. Miriam was the only woman in this trio who was called to lead two million Israelites from Egypt and through the wilderness (Micah 6:4). She was allowed the privilege of great authority and responsibility in ministry, as we will discover as we work our way through this session.

But is the authority and responsibility Miriam carried something now forbidden or discouraged for women? Are women in ministry living out of divine order? Does Scripture limit a woman's involvement in the church? Is a woman's ability to minister hindered due to her gender? You may already have strong opinions on the subject, or you may never have addressed the issue at all.

The questions surrounding women in ministry abound and are debated throughout the church. Though the Bible is neither contradictory nor vague on the subject, definitive conclusions are difficult to reach. Regardless, the question of women in church ministry involvement (especially in leadership roles) is valid, and deserves a thorough examination.

Read 1 Corinthians 12:4–11; Ephesians 4:11–16.

Questions:

Have you developed your own view of women in Christian ministry? What are those beliefs and what is the scriptural basis for them?

✎ _____

_____

_____

Is there anything in the Scripture passages listed above that leads you to distinguish between ministries available to men and women?

✎ _____

_____

_____

How does the fact that Miriam is listed in the Word of God as one sent by God to lead (Micah 6:4) affect your beliefs?

✎ _____

_____

_____

In what ways do you think modern feminism and chauvinism have affected the view of Christian ministry by women?

✎ _____

_____

_____

Kingdom Life—*Ministering Women*

Let us examine a woman's status and position before God as it relates to ministry. How does God view women, and does He consider them secondary to men?

In session two, we discovered how women's role in creation shifted after the fall (see page 13). To reiterate slightly, there is no evidence that God's designation of Adam as servant-leader was ever intended to be understood as a diminishing of a woman's person or giftedness. Rather, it is a redemptive role that opens the way to the fullest joy of her voluntary submission in the freedom of the true relationship God intended for husband and wife.

One need only look closely at the stories of Miriam, Deborah, Huldah, or Esther to see examples of women used mightily by God in positions of leadership and authority. It is quite evident in the Old Testament that God not only condoned, but blessed the sincere efforts of godly women in prominent spiritual leadership; He spoke to them and through them as well.

By the time of Christ, the view of women had seemingly darkened considerably from what it was in Miriam's day. A popular Jewish saying was, "Thank God that I am neither a Gentile, a slave, nor a woman." It was taught that women were incapable of receiving religious instruction, and a rabbi could not speak openly to a woman in public, even if she was his wife or sister. But Jesus burst upon the scene, casting a bright new light on God's intended purpose for women in His kingdom.

Read John 11—12:11; 20:15–18; Acts 1:13, 14; 2:14–21.

Questions:

At a time when friendships between men and women were disapproved of, what was Jesus' relationship not only with Lazarus, but with Mary and Martha?

To whom did Jesus first entrust the vital news of His resurrection?

_____

_____

_____

Who was present on the day of Pentecost?

_____

_____

_____

What is the spiritual status given to women in Acts 2:14–21?

_____

_____

_____

From what you've seen thus far, compose a list of words that would summarize Jesus' view and treatment of women during His earthly ministry (for example, compassionate, friendly).

_____

_____

_____

Did Christ's death and resurrection limit or change a woman's spiritual status?

_____

_____

_____

Does it appear a woman's potential in ministry was diminished or increased by the death and resurrection of Jesus and the giving of the Holy Spirit? Explain.

_____

_____

_____

Probing the Depths

It is safe to conclude, then, that a woman's freedom to minister is not restricted by God's view of her as a lesser creation, by any Old Testament precedent, or by some spiritual or other inherent limitation on her part.

If you want to gain valuable, biblical insight into the nature of leadership roles for men and women, a helpful resource may be found in *A Man's Starting Place*, by Jack W. Hayford, Regal Books, Ventura, CA.

Kingdom Life—*Kings and Priests*

Acts 2:17, 18 quotes the prophet Joel, "And it shall come to pass in the last days, says God, that I will pour out of my Spirit on all flesh; your sons and your daughters shall prophesy, your young men shall see visions, your old men shall dream dreams. And on My menservants and on My maidservants I will pour out My Spirit in those days; and they shall prophesy." The outpouring of the Spirit in the Old Testament had been largely reserved for the spiritual and national leaders of Israel. Under the New Covenant, however, the authority of the Spirit is for "all flesh," all who come under the New Covenant. Every believer, male and female, young and old, is anointed to be a priest and king to God (Revelation 1:6).

This fact is seen throughout the New Testament in the lives of many godly women who served as leaders in the infant church. Phoebe (Romans 16:1, 2) was not only a servant of the church, but a helper (in other versions this word is translated as servant, deaconess, or minister) of many. According to many scholars, it was Phoebe who carried the written book of Romans to the congregation. Priscilla co-labored with her husband as one of the first missionary couples in the Christian church. This couple is referenced seven times in Scripture; in many of those seven, Priscilla is mentioned first. Many believe this is because she was the more active and outspoken of the two. It is even believed by some scholars (though most disagree) that Priscilla may have authored the book of Hebrews. Phillip's four unmarried daughters were powerful New Testament prophets. Acts 21:8, 9 makes it clear that women did bring God's word by the power of the Holy Spirit and that such ministry was fully accepted in the early church. The list could go on.

Read Romans 8:14–17; Ephesians 1:7–14; 4:11–16.

Questions:

Old Testament culture demanded an inheritance be passed only to males. Since these verses obviously apply to men and women, what does their message mean to New Covenant women?

_____

_____

As an heir of Christ, what things has He provided for you as a woman of faith?

_____

_____

Is there any indication that the leadership gifts listed in Ephesians 4:11 are reserved for men?

_____

_____

Taking the preceding section into account, what do you see as limitations on women as leaders in the New Testament church?

_____

_____

In what way(s), if any, has this section changed your view of leadership and ministry by women?

_____

_____

_____

Word Wealth—*Equipping*

Equipping, *katartismos* (kat-ar-tis-moss'); Strong's #2677: A making fit, preparing, training, perfecting, making fully qualified for service. In classical language, the word is used for setting a bone during surgery. The Great Physician is now working through His men and women within the church, making all the necessary adjustments so the church will be whole and functioning as a healthy, vibrant entity.

Kingdom Extra

A well-known Christian author, entertainer, and speaker (who was married with children) was asked how she dealt with the many demands on her time. Her reply was so simple, yet so immensely profound. She said, "Well, I have my devotions every day. I minister to God, and He gives to me. Out of that, I minister to the needs of my husband. Then I minister to my children by caring for their needs. And with whatever time I have left, I minister to the body of Christ."

This woman had her priorities straight. She obviously understood the principle in effect in Titus 2:3–5. In this passage, older women are exhorted to assume the responsibilities of their new position in the gospel. These include providing a proper example for the young women and teaching them Christian character and domestic responsibilities. To disregard husband, family, and duties of a wife and mother would be an abuse of the freedom found in Christ.

Read Proverbs 31:10–31; 1 Timothy 3:8–12.

Questions:

What seem to be the Proverbs 31 woman's priorities? In what order?

✎ _____

_____

_____

With this model of prioritizing in mind, what must be true of our lives before our ministry reaches beyond our own homes?

✎ _____

_____

_____

Being totally honest, list those things to which you give your time in any given week and assign the number of hours you devote to each. What changes need to happen in order for you to live out the Proverbs 31 model?

✎ _____

_____

_____

According to Paul, what are the prerequisites to ministry outside the home?

✎ _____

_____

_____

Probing the Depths

Not all the issues pertaining to women in ministry are as clear-cut as those addressed thus far. First Corinthians 14:26–40 is a difficult passage to understand where this subject is concerned. Take some time to read this passage.

It will aid our grasp of this passage to look at why Paul wrote this letter in the first place. Paul established the church at Corinth about A.D. 50–51 and continued to carry on correspondence and exercise care for the church after his departure. The first letter to the Corinthian church reveals some of the typical Greek cultural problems of Paul's day, including the gross sexual immorality of the city of Corinth. The Greeks were known for their idolatry, divisive philosophies, spirit of litigation, and rejection of the bodily resurrection. The city was infamous for its sensuality and sacred prostitution. The spirit of the city showed up in the church and explains the kind of problems the people faced.

The speculation as to why Paul made the address of 14:34, 35 is vast. One view is that the women had been allocated to a separate court in the Jewish temples, so full participation in worship was a new experience. They were curious and asking questions during the meeting (v. 35). Another view is that Paul was addressing an issue of respect. The women, in their emancipated role, were taking issue with the men over what was being taught, and in doing so, were usurping authority and shaming their husbands in public. (Note: the Greek word for "woman" can also mean "wife.") The best interpretation is probably to see Paul as prohibiting undisciplined discussion that would disturb the service rather than forbidding women to manifest spiritual gifts in the service.

Kingdom Life—*Facing the Giant*

When it comes to the controversy regarding women in ministry, one passage rises head and shoulders above all others. It is seen by many as a warning and by others as the verification of a suspected fact. First Timothy 2:11, 12 have been the source of seemingly unending debates and have many times been used to hinder effective kingdom ministry. Take time now to read 1 Timothy 2:8–15.

We must first realize the purpose of Paul's letter. Timothy was a very young man who had been entrusted with the task of leading an infant church. Begun by Paul, the young church had started well, but had fallen into a mess. Apparently, the religion of Ephesian culture had infiltrated the gospel of Christ and threatened to destroy the church. This tendency toward returning to idolatry, coupled with a religious spirit that loved debate but had little time for God, had created a polluted mess. And young Timothy was called on to set things right. His was the task of speaking healthy words of wisdom to counteract the sinful attitudes that had developed in the Ephesian church.

The Ephesian Christians had come from a spiritual history of goddess worship—they worshipped Diana, the goddess of the hunt, the moon, and birthing. She was believed to be a virgin goddess who especially looked after women. It is not hard to imagine that, in such a female-honoring culture, the women had become quite aggressive and assertive. Add to that the fact that false teachers had arisen and had been polluting the gospel of Christ, and you have a recipe for disaster.

Timothy was called to teach and lead these confused, misled, baby Christians back to the pure truth of the gospel.

Read 1 Timothy 2:8–15 again.

Questions:

Taking the worship of Diana and the subsequent female-oriented society of Ephesus into consideration, what situations may have arisen in worship services that prompted Paul's words to Timothy?

✎ _____

_____

By nature, Eve was more trusting than Adam and was thereby deceived. Adam, on the other hand, sinned by deliberate choice. With these facts in mind, how might we understand Paul's words regarding Eve (1 Timothy 2:13, 14)?

✎ _____

_____

What intrinsic qualities of women in general make them susceptible to deception?

✎ _____

_____

_____

Taking this passage from 1 Timothy in light of all we have studied thus far, what now is your understanding of Paul's words?

✎ _____

_____

_____

Record Your Thoughts

It is important to note that this study is not intended to provide reasons for women to stay home and avoid ministry or leave home to pursue it. All aspects of our lives are subject to the fine scrutiny of Scripture to ensure our obedience to God's purpose at every season. Our pursuit of ministry, or any other goal, should not be based on personal ambition or desire, but subject to God's order for our lives, families, and His church.

SESSION FIVE

Miriam, Daughter Who Spoke

 Kingdom Key—*Guard Your Tongue*

Matthew 12:36, 37 But I say to you that for every idle word men may speak, they will give account of it in the day of judgment. For by your words you will be justified, and by your words you will be condemned.

In Old Testament times, God considered the power of the tongue of such importance that a trespass offering had to be given for speaking thoughtlessly (Leviticus 5:4–6). In the Scripture passage above, Jesus Christ had some very strong words to say about the words we speak— His words should give us all pause.

Our words are very powerful and can build or destroy lives. This is why God views our words with such high priority. Our words can build up or tear down. They can indelibly affect individual lives, marriages, communities, and nations. Words can inflict damage in invisible yet enduring ways upon speaker and hearer alike; they can lead to lasting benefit or permanent loss. They can give forth the power of life or speak darkness and death into the world around us.

Read Psalm 119:11; James 3:2–12; Luke 6:45.

Questions:

Consider yesterday. Think carefully about the words you spoke, even if no one but you heard them. Were they words of life, or words of darkness and death? Why do you think this is so?

✎ _____

_____

_____

What steps can you take to ensure the words you speak build up and benefit others?

✎ _____

_____

_____

How can your negative words affect you just as much as, if not more than, the ones to whom you speak?

✎ _____

_____

_____

 Word Wealth—*Idle*

Idle, *argos* (ar-gos'), Strong's #692: useless, barren, yielding no return, thoughtless, profitless, inactive, lazy, or unemployed. As used in Matthew 12:36, it implies an act devoid of caring. Words used without thought or proper attention can often inflict more damage than words chosen specifically to offend. When one tries to offend, at least the other person is considered worthy of attention. When one speaks without any thought to the hearer, it points to a cold and careless heart.

Kingdom Life—*Anointed, Not Perfected*

Miriam was truly anointed and gifted of God as a ministering woman. She was a strong worship leader and the first woman in Scripture to be honored with the title "prophetess" (Exodus 15:20, 21). Miriam was fiercely loyal, and extremely patriotic to the cause of the Israelite nation.

Interestingly, the giftings of God can often have both positive and negative expression through the lives of human (and therefore, sinful) vessels. Those areas where one is most gifted can, at the same time, be areas in which one is most prone to failure. We see one of the clearest instances of this in the life of Miriam. She was a gifted leader and spokesperson, but she began to think that she was qualified for more authority than God had apportioned for her. Unfortunately, she put words to her thoughts.

Turn to Numbers 12:1–16 and read the account of Miriam's failure. Aaron joined her in questioning Moses' authority. It is interesting to note the order in which their names appear.

It is doubtful that Miriam and Aaron were criticizing Moses' wife because of her race as an Ethiopian; more likely, it was because she was not one of the people of the covenant. We do see precedent for this in other places in Scripture. In Genesis 24:37, Abraham is specific in his request that Isaac not take a bride from the Canaanites. Also, the Ethiopians (Cushites) were a heathen and idolatrous nation. Exodus 34:10–16 makes it clear that the Israelites were not to covenant with idolatrous peoples for fear they would become participants in the idolatrous practices.

Read Proverbs 11:1–6; 29:23; Isaiah 29:19–21; 57:15; James 4:6, 10, 11; 1 Peter 5:6–10.

Questions:

In your opinion, why is the fact that Moses was a humble man inserted in the account of Miriam and Aaron's rebellion?

It is said, "A situation does not make the person; it reveals the person." What was revealed about Miriam? What heart attitude led her to question Moses' authority?

✎_____

_____

_____

Pride is the opposite of humility. What do you believe is the meaning of "God resists the proud"?

✎_____

_____

_____

When in your own life have you experienced the spiritual infirmity and separation from God caused by a prideful spirit?

✎_____

_____

_____

In reading Numbers 12:1–16, what is the progression of events that led to Miriam's healing and reinstatement into the camp?

✎_____

_____

_____

What can this progression teach us about the proper and healing steps to take in our own lives when sin has separated us from fellowship with God?

✎_____

_____

_____

Kingdom Extra

Numbers 12:1–16 relates how Moses' sister, Miriam, was healed of leprosy. She received physical healing through the intercession of Aaron and Moses. However, her healing was delayed seven days because of her sin in defying the God-given leadership of Moses.

Is it possible that delays in receiving answers to our prayer may sometimes be the result of a sinful attitude? Is there instruction in the fact that the progress of the whole camp was delayed until Miriam was restored? Repentance and humility will not earn healing, but they may—as with Miriam—clear the way for God's grace to be revealed more fully (1 Corinthians 12:20–27).

Behind the Scenes

The Law of Moses and cultural realities are an integral part of the scene played out between God, Moses, Aaron, and Miriam.

Spitting in the face was a sign of contempt in Old Testament times (Deuteronomy 25:9). God had shown His contempt of Miriam's attitude and actions just as surely as an earthly father might show contempt by spitting in his child's face.

Also, Miriam was "shut out of the camp seven days" (Numbers 12:14). Seven days is the length of elapsed time prescribed for the priest's first and second inspections of leprosy victims (Leviticus 13). The implication is that she was healed in response to Moses' prayer and would be pronounced clean after seven days.

Kingdom Life—*Watch Your Words*

God has given us, His unique creation, the gift and power of speech. From our mouths can flow life-affirming words or we can speak forth words that tear down and spread darkness. We learned earlier in this session that we will be held accountable for even the idle (or thoughtless) words we speak.

We must realize that capacity and ability constitute accountability and responsibility. We should never be pleased to dwell on a level of existence lower than that on which God has made it possible for us to dwell. We should strive to be the best we can be and to reach the highest levels we can reach. To do less is to be unfaithful stewards of the gift entrusted to us and we may even be used by our enemy in his battle against God's people.

In 2 Corinthians 2:11, the Bible warns that we should not be ignorant of Satan's devices, lest he take advantage of (use) us. Through the spoken word, Miriam became a tool in the enemy's hand to try and destroy one of God's chosen leaders. (For further reading, see Genesis 39 to learn how Potiphar's wife was similarly used against Joseph.)

Read Proverbs 18:21; 27:19; Matthew 12:34; James 3:1–12.

Questions:

What does the Bible say our words reveal?

_____

_____

_____

What does the verse in Proverbs tell us the heart reveals?

_____

_____

_____

How do our words have power?

_____

_____

_____

How can you be a faithful steward of the gift entrusted to you: your speech?

✏️ _____

_____

_____

Problems with the mouth are directly related to the problems of the heart—a heart in need of transformation. Give the scriptural basis for this truth. How can our hearts be transformed? List the Bible passages that answer this question.

✏️ _____

_____

_____

How can these truths lead us to a place wherein we can "bridle" our tongues?

✏️ _____

_____

_____

Kingdom Life—*In His Image*

God is a creative being, who made and upholds all things by the power of His Word. We were made in His image. Obviously, we do not possess the omnipresence, omnipotence, or all-powerful might of God within ourselves. But, like God, man is not only body, but also soul and spirit—he is, in his essence, a spiritual being. He is also a moral being whose intelligence, perception, and self-determination far exceed that of any other earthly being.

As such, man has the ability and responsibility of interacting with and influencing people and situations around him. As we have seen, the words that proceed from our mouths have an innate ability to bring life or death into our surroundings. God spoke creation into existence; our power is not that of creating something from nothing, but of enhancing those people or situations our lives touch. We can build upon God's "something" or we can destroy—we can attempt to create nothing (idle words that tear down) from something (the grandeur of God's creation).

Read Proverbs 15:18–33; Ecclesiastes 5:2, 3; Ephesians 4:25–32; 5:1–19; Colossians 4:6; James 3:13–18.

Questions:

Can you recall a time when your words created nothing from something? What was the outcome?

_____

_____

_____

What do you believe caused you to make such disparaging decisions in your dealings with others?

_____

_____

_____

Can you recall a time when your words enhanced a person or situation? What was the outcome?

_____

_____

_____

What godly directives are contained in the passages above that will help you guard your words and speak life rather than death?

_____

_____

_____

Consider the relationship between wisdom and a guarded tongue. What steps can you take to increase your ability to speak life?

✎ _____

_____

_____

What is required of the one who would choose to speak life?

✎ _____

_____

_____

What part do emotions play in the decision to speak life? What part does obedience play in that decision?

✎ _____

_____

_____

Look back over this lesson thus far, and write a summary of why your words have power. What has most inspired or challenged you so far?

✎ _____

_____

_____

Kingdom Extra

There are innumerable scripture references that reveal the dangers and problems stemming from idle, life-negating talk, as well as the life-begetting power in the tongue. A good place to gain further insight is in the Book of Proverbs. You might want to read one chapter a day for the next month and underline each verse that relates to the tongue, the heart, or the words of the mouth.

James 3:1–12 makes it obvious that James had strong feelings about the power of the tongue! It is true "the tongue is a little member" (v. 5), but its power and influence for good or bad are out of proportion to its size. Now look at James 3:8. From this verse, it appears the tongue is not tamable. But is it possible to "bridle the tongue"? Can we control what we say with our mouths and how we say it? James doesn't lay out much hope.

However, the Bible never tells us to do anything that the Lord does not give us the strength to accomplish (1 Corinthians 10:13; Philippians 4:13). Even James concedes "these things ought not to be so" (James 3:10); therefore, it must be possible, by God's grace, to tame the tongue.

A powerful key to taming the tongue can be found in Romans 12:1 and 2: "I beseech you therefore, brethren, by the mercies of God, that you present your bodies a living sacrifice, holy, acceptable to God, which is your reasonable service. And do not be conformed to this world, but be transformed by the renewing of your mind, that you may prove what is that good and acceptable and perfect will of God.

Word Wealth—*Conformed*

Conformed, *suschematizo* (soos-khay-mat-id'-doe); Strong's #4964: *Suschematizo* refers to conforming oneself in outer fashion or outward appearance, or to accommodating oneself to a model or pattern. *Suschematizo* occurs only once more in the New Testament—1 Peter 1:14—where it describes those conforming themselves to worldly lusts. Even apparent or superficial conformity to the present world system or any accommodation to its ways could be fatal to the Christian life.

Word Wealth—*Transformed*

Transformed, *metamorphoo* (met-am-or-fo'-o); Strong's #3339: *Metamorphoo* is a verb meaning to change to another form. This is the word used of Christ's transfiguration (Matthew 17:2; Mark 9:2). In Romans 12:2, it speaks of a believer's obligation to undergo a complete change, under the power of God, which will find expression in character and conduct. The word stresses inner change and communicates a continuous, ongoing process.

Jesus makes it clear that "out of the abundance of the heart the mouth speaks" (Matthew 12:34). So it should be obvious to one who would tame the tongue that the issues of the heart are of prime importance. In order for our words to be seasoned with love and life, we must be transformed from the heart outward.

The Word of God illuminated by the Holy Spirit is the only true means for transforming the human heart. Salvation by faith is a specific occasion, while the renewing of the mind by the Word is a continuing process. The disciple devotes himself to God's Word to be transformed into a holy person, radiantly Christlike, and radically different from the world. Spiritual disciples devour God's Word because in it is the key to a more dynamic relationship with their living Lord and a greater availability to the Holy Spirit.

Read Proverbs 16:23; Ephesians 4:17, 22–32; 5:19, 20; Romans 10:17; Hebrews 4:12; James 3:2.

Questions:

Apparently, we are able to control what we say. Why do you think our tongues are such stumbling blocks?

What is your understanding of a renewed mind?

What role does God's Word have in the renewing of our minds (hearts)?

What does it mean to "put off the old man?"

✎ _____

_____

What does the Word of God do within the one who partakes of its riches?

✎ _____

_____

_____

Kingdom Life—*Change Your Mind*

Did you know you are right now in the process of transformation? As you are reading and studying God's Word, He is revealing to you the intentions of your heart (Hebrews 4:12). As you submit those intentions to His lordship and commit yourself to His ways, your heart will become more like His. God renews the mind (heart) through His Word.

But a wise believer will be diligent in protecting and guarding against being re-polluted by the things of the world. Philippians 4:6–8 promises God's peace—a peace that "surpasses all understanding." God's peace acts as a guard against the pollution of worldly thinking, acting, and speaking. When peace fills our hearts and minds, we are not easily tempted toward reactionary thinking or impulsive action.

Read Psalm 29:11; 119:165; Isaiah 26:3; 48:18; Romans 8:5–9; 14:17, 18; Colossians 3:14–17.

Questions:

How can we receive the peace of God?

✎ _____

_____

_____

How can the peace of God keep us from stumbling in our walk of faith?

_____

_____

_____

In what way can peace be "like a river"?

_____

_____

_____

What do you believe it means to be "spiritually minded"?

_____

_____

_____

From what you have learned thus far in this section, what do you see as the relationship between God's Word, His peace, and our ability to live successful lives of faith?

_____

_____

_____

Word Wealth—*Guard*

Guard, *phroureo* (froo-reh'-o); Strong's #5432: A military term picturing a sentry standing guard as protection against the enemy. We are in spiritual combat, but God's power and peace are our sentinels and protectors.

Record Your Thoughts

Once your thoughts are under captive obedience, what then? Turn to Philippians 4:8, 9 and read it once again. Write the eight key words that convey the things you *are* to think about.

It is imperative to those who would live an effective, powerful life of faith to realize character and conduct begin in the mind. Your actions are affected by the things upon which you focus your thoughts. Paul cautions us to concentrate on things that will result in right living and in God's peace. To further your journey toward a healthy, peaceful, powerful life in God's kingdom, spend time dwelling on the list from Philippians 4:8 and take your needs in those areas to the Lord. Ask Him to give you a greater desire for His Word and to fill your heart and mind with the peace only He can give.

It is important to remember that the transforming of your mind is a continual process, not a one-time occurrence. It requires the *daily* maintenance of bringing your petitions to God and feeding upon His Word. Remain faithful, and you'll be amazed by your progress!

SESSION SIX

Deborah, Wise Leader

 Kingdom Key—*Great Commission in Action*

Matthew 5:13–16 You are the salt of the earth; but if the salt loses its flavor, how shall it be seasoned? It is then good for nothing but to be thrown out and trampled underfoot by men. You are the light of the world. A city that is set on a hill cannot be hidden. Nor do they light a lamp and put it under a basket, but on a lampstand, and it gives light to all *who are* in the house. Let your light so shine before men, that they may see your good works and glorify your Father in heaven.

The Beatitudes of Jesus describe the essential character of kingdom citizens, and the metaphors of "salt" and "light" indicate the influence God's people can have in penetrating secular society with the truth of the gospel. In this way, we are kingdom leaders—leading others to the cross of Christ.

Leadership is not a responsibility afforded to only a few, but a privilege given by God to all. For leading is simply guiding or influencing the way of another. And Jesus asked every believer to participate in showing others the way to eternal life (Acts 1:8).

So whether it is across the sea or across the street, as a state senator or a team mom, as a corporate executive or a PTA committee member, we have all been given the opportunity to lead and influence others, and to help them find their way to The Way, Jesus Christ.

Read Matthew 5:2–16; John 15:1–17; Philippians 2:1–16; 1 Peter 2:11, 12.

Questions:

In what ways do you now see yourself as a leader in the kingdom of God?

✎ _____

_____

_____

What are some practical ways you can be "salt" and "light" in your daily life?

✎ _____

_____

_____

What does it mean to "abide" in Christ?

✎ _____

_____

_____

What "fruit" can be expected to grow in the life of one firmly connected to Jesus, the True Vine?

✎ _____

_____

_____

What attitude of heart must we cultivate in our lives to truly be a "light" to others?

✎ _____

_____

_____

In what ways can pride be detrimental to our witness to the world?

_____

_____

_____

In what ways can pride be detrimental to our own walk of faith?

_____

_____

_____

What is "honorable" behavior for those who profess Christ as Lord?

_____

_____

_____

Kingdom Life—*Gifted to Serve*

To prepare for the remainder of this session, read chapters 4 and 5 of Judges.

Deborah (whose name means "Honeybee") was raised up by God as a female judge and prophetess in ancient Israel. Her multiple leadership functions demonstrate the possibilities for any woman who will allow God's Spirit to fill and form her life.

Deborah became a celebrated leader of political influence and authority, while maintaining the grace and dignity of womanhood. She also acquired a reputation as a wise arbitrator of justice, counselor, wife, and deliverer in time of war. Her successful mobilization of the Israelite militia demonstrated her leadership ability and spiritual insight.

As a model of a woman leader, Deborah depicts the finest possibilities of a gifted, God-fearing woman who allows the Spirit of God to develop her full capacities to impact the world around her.

Read Ephesians 4:11–16; Romans 12:4–8; 13:1.

Questions:

Does anything in the passages listed above limit ministry to only male members of the body of Christ?

_____

_____

Where do you believe the doctrine of male-only leadership began?

_____

_____

_____

What is your current view of this doctrine?

_____

_____

_____

With the passages above in mind, what are the giftings that God brings into His church?

_____

_____

_____

What is the purpose of those giftings?

_____

_____

_____

Who is the recipient of those giftings?

_____

_____

What giftings do you possess with which to serve the body of Christ and lead others to the saving cross of Christ?

_____

_____

_____

Behind the Scenes

The Book of Judges covers a chaotic period in Israel's history from about 1380 to 1050 B.C. Under the leadership of Joshua, Israel had generally conquered and occupied the land of Canaan, but large areas remained yet to be possessed by the individual tribes. Israel did evil in the sight of the Lord continually and "there was no king in Israel; everyone did what was right in his own eyes" (Judges 21:25). By deliberately serving foreign gods, the people of Israel broke their covenant with the Lord. As a result, the Lord delivered them into the hands of various oppressors. Each time the people cried out to the Lord, He faithfully raised up a judge to bring deliverance to His people. These judges, whom the Lord chose and anointed with His Spirit, were military and civil leaders.

Kingdom Life—*Called to Serve*

Deborah had a definite calling from God, and He raised her up and enabled her to fulfill that call as she responded to His will. God has also called each one of us to lead, through whatever sphere of influence we're afforded.

Because few of us will sit as a judge over a nation or hold positions of vast influence, we may minimize our individual callings or feel we are insignificant in God's kingdom. But it is clear you *are* called by Him for a purpose and should never feel ashamed of your role or diminished by the sphere of influence you possess. To reinvent a well-known phrase: there are no small ministries, only small ministers.

If we are ever tempted to think we don't have what it takes to be called by God, we must turn to the Word of God and remind ourselves of our established place in His kingdom and His plan. *All* believers are called by God and chosen for His purpose.

Read Romans 8:29, 30; 1 Corinthians 12:12–31; Ephesians 2:10.

Questions:

What is the one unarguable fact contained in all the passages listed above?

_____

_____

_____

What do you believe is the source of questions we face regarding the validity of our giftings or place in the body of Christ?

_____

_____

_____

What are the gifts God has entrusted to you? How can you make better use of the gifts you've been given?

_____

_____

_____

What steps can you take to enable you to be a more effective minister in the kingdom?

_____

_____

_____

Kingdom Extra

The human body is an exquisite organism. Scientists cannot duplicate it or even fully understand it. It is a synthesis of many parts all working together in a comprehensive whole. What affects one part of the body affects the whole. Each member of the body relates to and depends upon other parts of the body. Each contributes to the welfare of the entire body. The same is true of all believers as members of the body of Christ. We should function in Christ's body as the parts of the human body function in it. There is no Christian brother or sister whom we do not need.

Word Wealth—*Body*

Body, *soma* (so'-mah); Strong's #4983: *Soma* is the body as a sound whole. It is the instrument of life. The Greek word *soma* is related to *sozo*, meaning to heal, preserve, be made whole. This clearly shows how our lives are inextricably woven together within the body of Christ, and how our well-being depends upon the well-being of others (Romans 14:7). Let us allow Christ to knit us together in His church.

Kingdom Life—*Called to a Committed Life*

In Judges 4:4, Deborah is called a prophetess, as was Miriam (Exodus 15:20). She was also a judge, a recognized office of both national and spiritual leadership. This required her to render decisions on peoples' inquiries at a time when they sought reasons for their oppression (Judges 4:3).

Deborah's ability to discern the mind and purposes of God was not something she could have acquired overnight. We can only surmise from her spiritual maturity as an adult that she sought hard after God as a young woman; only quality time spent in the presence of God can bring forth the wisdom we see in the life of Deborah. She had to have been a woman totally sold out to a life of continual growth and service to the Lord.

Deborah's commitment was built on a solid foundation and only grew stronger with time.

She was committed to the ways of the Lord, the people of the Lord, and, most importantly, to the Person of the Lord God.

Read Micah 6:8; Psalm 15; 84:10–12; Proverbs 2:1–9; 15:21–24; Isaiah 33:15, 16.

Questions:

What traits do you believe could be seen in one who lives out the words of Micah 6:8?

_____

_____

_____

With these passages in mind, what is your understanding of the word "upright?"

_____

_____

Consider your own life in light of these passages. What areas do you see in which you fail to live "uprightly"?

_____

_____

_____

What can you do to receive greater enabling to walk faithfully and with wisdom in these areas of your life?

_____

_____

_____

Spend some time looking up Bible passages that speak of godly wisdom. From where can wisdom be gained? What are the benefits of wisdom?

_____

_____

_____

Probing the Depths

Proverbs 16:23, 24 make it clear that what God's wisdom (His Word) has taught our hearts—those truths and promises—are to influence our speech. Wisdom's fruit should transmit our knowledge to our lips. The Word in our hearts should affect, teach, and control our speech and conduct. The "sweetness" and "health" such speech promotes are desirable, whether in our human relationships or in the release of divine grace in our daily living. God's wisdom planted deeply within the hearts of believers leads them to an overcoming, victorious life, through consistent acknowledgement of the power and might of God with both mouth and manner.

Kingdom Life—*Called to Count the Cost*

Deborah was a called and committed leader, but neither of those came without a willingness to embrace the cost demanded of those who will serve without limitation, without fear, without regret, and without turning back when the going gets tough.

Jesus made it clear that those who will be effective disciples in His kingdom must subordinate self-will to His will. A disciple must die to self-centeredness and be willing to endure whatever life may bring in the cause of carrying the light of the gospel of Christ.

Discipleship means the total renunciation of all selfish interest for the sake of Jesus. Our commitment to the Lord must be total and without any shadow of turning if we are to experience the maximum realization of Christ's purpose for our lives.

Read Luke 14:25–33.

Questions:

What do you think Jesus' words in Luke 14:26 mean to us as children of God called to a life of love and service?

✎ _____

_____

In what way is constructing a building an object lesson in living a committed life of faith?

✎ _____

_____

_____

In what ways can the example of a king who considers going to war further our understanding of the commitment required of those who would serve the Lord with their lives?

✎ _____

_____

_____

In an honest appraisal of your own life, do you see this type of commitment in action?

✎ _____

_____

_____

What prevents you from making the type of commitment to the Lord's service that we see in Deborah?

✎ _____

_____

Kingdom Life—*Called to Confident and Courageous Faith*

Deborah's faith in God and confidence of His purpose was unswerving. She was a bold and confident leader, but her effectiveness was not born out of her great abilities or natural wisdom. It stemmed from her relationship with God and what she knew He was capable of doing through a willing vessel. She was no doubt aware of the mighty exploits of those God had used before her, including Moses and Joshua, and her confidence showed she believed all she had heard about the great Yahweh. She knew Him to be faithful and true to His people—enough so for her to act upon it. Deborah's confidence and strength were admirably balanced with a receptive humility, totally void of arrogance or pride as witnessed by her attentiveness to the Lord's leading and her willingness to immediately obey. Hers was a brave heart willing to initiate action against the forces opposed to God's purposes for His people. Deborah knew the Spirit behind their mission was far greater than any opposition they could face. She had the courage to believe God would deliver the enemy into their hands, as He had promised.

Read 1 Samuel 17:47; Isaiah 54:17; Romans 8:31–39; 2 Corinthians 10:3–5.

Questions:

We are promised that the "battle is the Lord's." What does that mean to you in your everyday life?

_____

_____

_____

The Lord promises to bring to nothing those things that would seek to defeat you. What specifically are the things in your life that threaten to overtake you?

_____

_____

_____

How can you be more than a conqueror over those things?

_____

_____

_____

With these passages in mind, what place should fear have in the life of one called to be a light to the world and lead others to saving faith in Christ?

_____

_____

_____

How can you overcome fear and doubt?

_____

_____

_____

_____

Kingdom Extra

Is there a point in your own life where a battle is raging? Is there a strategy of the enemy operating in opposition to the purpose and will of God for you? Take courage! The Lord is on your side. He is willing and able to deliver. You are _more_ than a conqueror in Christ (Romans 8:37–39). Choose to align yourself with Him, according to the provisions of His Word (Deuteronomy 7:1–26). Then take the authority He has given you in prayer, resist the enemy by renouncing his works, and watch him flee (James 4:7)!

Record Your Thoughts

Although we have not taken time to fully explore completely the seven qualities of leadership we see in Deborah's life, each has been touched upon by this session. The qualities seen in a godly leader are:

- they are called;
- they are committed;
- they count the cost before they step forward;
- they have been enabled by God—they have the capacity for leadership;
- they are confident;
- they are courageous and operate in a strong conviction of truth and purpose.

To secure in your understanding the seven qualities of leadership Deborah exhibited, review this lesson and consider each point, particularly as it relates to every believer who is willing to be led by God and to lead others for His glory.

Do you see these qualities in your own life? In what ways?

_____

_____

_____

How do you see God using you as a light to influence the world around you?

_____

_____

_____

What steps can you take to make yourself more available to the Lord and more effective in affecting the world for Him?

_____

_____

_____

ADDITIONAL OBSERVATIONS

SESSION SEVEN

Ruth, Daughter of Faithfulness

 Kingdom Key—*Faithful Service*

Luke 16:10 He who is faithful in what is least is faithful also in much; and he who is unjust in what is least is unjust also in much.

As daughters of the Almighty God, we desire with all our hearts to serve Him. Yet we may feel limited by our situations in life, thinking all the really great and important things are being done by others, and that we have somehow been relegated to the eternally mundane. But only God knows the importance of the small daily acts of service done without recognition or fanfare.

Jesus Himself spent many years toiling faithfully in a carpenter's shop; and He reminded us on three separate occasions about our faithfulness in the small things being the key to the release of bigger things (Matthew 25:21; Luke 16:10; 19:17). In this lesson, we will examine the life of a woman who displayed great faithfulness in spite of difficult circumstances, and how that allowed the sovereign hand of God to move on her behalf.

Read the Book of Ruth.

Questions:

In what ways can you see Ruth being faithful in small things?

In looking at your own life, do you face daily challenges with the same amount of faithful service?

✎ _____

_____

_____

What do you believe motivates one who is faithful in even the mundane issues of life?

✎ _____

_____

_____

What attitude of heart enables the kind of faithfulness we see displayed in Ruth's life?

✎ _____

_____

_____

Reread Ruth 1:16, 17. What do you believe lies at the heart of Ruth's unswerving commitment to Naomi?

✎ _____

_____

_____

Behind the Scenes

The story contained in the Book of Ruth opens somewhere between 1150 and 1100 B.C., during the period of the Judges. Turn to Judges 2 and 3 and read of the conditions of the Israelites during this period of history.

In Ruth 1:1–5, we read of a famine that caused Elimelech (Naomi's husband and Ruth's father-in-law) and his family to depart Judah and move to Moab. The famine (1:1) was the natural by-product of sin, a judgment imposed by the people upon themselves through their disobedience. The Lord had previously warned that the land itself would turn against them if they were unfaithful to Him (Deuteronomy 28:15, 16, 23, 24, 38–40). Further, Elimelech's choice to move his family to the country of Moab (Ruth 1:2) is not evidenced as being God's direction but simply his own decision.

Moab was an evil and perverse land filled with idolatry and the Moabites were long-standing enemies of God's people, Israel. For obvious reasons, the two cultures clashed along many social and political lines.

The impact of Naomi's life upon her daughter-in-law was strong enough to cause Ruth to turn her back on her cursed heritage and her idolatrous upbringing and allow the hand of God to touch her heart. By watching Naomi's faith in action, Ruth became sensitive to the things of God.

You can answer further background and cultural questions related to the Book of Ruth by reading Numbers 22—31 and Deuteronomy 23:3, 4. You may also wish to consult study Bibles, reference books, or Bible concordances and encyclopedias. Understanding clearly the heritage Ruth left behind makes her faithful commitment even more impressive.

Kingdom Extra

The way we live before those God has placed in our lives can have a powerful and lasting impact. We are all living sermons about our Father and His kingdom. It is imperative we consider carefully the choices we make and the reactions we exhibit. We cannot be false in our walk with the Lord or be disingenuous, professing what is not truly alive in our hearts; but we must be genuine, wise servants who continually uphold our Master's kingdom rule and our own unswerving commitment to Him.

Read Proverbs 22:24, 25; 1 Timothy 4:12; Titus 2:7, 8; 1 Peter 2:11–25.

Questions:

What is the major message of these passages?

✎ _____

_____

_____

In what way is every action and reaction a choice?

✎ _____

_____

_____

Do you take time to consider the effect of your choices on others before you act or react? Explain.

✎ _____

_____

_____

How can having the Word of God planted deeply in your heart enable you to make wiser choices in your daily life?

✎ _____

_____

_____

Kingdom Life—*Maintain Confidence in God*

Though Elimelech sought to find refuge for his family by leaving his homeland behind, Moab was not the haven Elimelech had hoped it would be. Though his sons found wives there, the entire family experienced much pain and loss.

The devastating events left Naomi battered, discouraged, and life-worn. We read how Naomi felt "the hand of the LORD has gone out against me" (Ruth 1:13). While Naomi's perspective is understandable, her reaction should not be construed as a commentary either on the nature of God or on the actual cause of her condition. Very simply, Naomi had suffered much and experienced a crisis of faith. (To understand more about the types of difficulties Naomi may have experienced, both in her native Judah and in Moab, read Judges 6:1–10.)

Though Naomi was a bit bitter and discouraged, she maintained a conviction, however strained, of God's kindness, goodness, and constancy. This can be seen in Ruth 1:8 wherein Naomi used the name "Yahweh" (translated in Scripture as Lord) in referring to God. This name is a very personal, intimate name for God and speaks of Naomi's continued trust in Him and commitment to follow Him even though she struggled to understand His ways. Naomi knew Yahweh's character and prayed her daughters-in-law would experience His goodness. It is obvious in her words to them that she recognized the God of Israel is not only kind, but also dependable.

Read Psalm 42.

Questions:

What can we learn from Naomi's words to her daughters-in-law that can help us when we feel life makes no sense and is too difficult to face?

✎ _____

_____

_____

The writer of Psalm 42 experienced the same type of struggle Naomi faced in feeling discouraged and overwhelmed by life. According to what is revealed in this psalm, what helps did he employ to rise above his circumstance and trust in God's goodness?

✎ _____

_____

_____

How can you employ these same helps when life's trouble strikes?

Kingdom Extra

When life brings hardship and we find ourselves depressed, desperate, and down, Psalm 42 encourages us to hope in God. The psalmist reminds himself of God's faithfulness and power. He determines to take control of his own attitude and praise God for who He is rather than question Him as a result of circumstance. This determination to praise in the midst of trouble is the very heart of worship.

Worshippers are assured by this insightful psalm that God will "help" them with His "countenance." The word "countenance" references to more than the physical face of God; it incorporates the evidence of the feeling or attitude of the seeker. It refers to the appearance and the attention. It creates a picture of the seeker with an upturned face, heart and eyes focused with full attention. It conveys the expectation and certainty that God's caring countenance will turn toward the one who praises, and the praiser's countenance is lifted by His present love.

Kingdom Life—*Selfless Loyalty*

Read Ruth 1:6–22 again.

Naomi's pain and discouragement is almost tangible to the reader. She had lost almost all that was precious to her and had decided to leave Moab and return to the land of Judah, where her God was worshiped and where she likely had many friends. But she had decided first to release her daughters-in-law (Ruth and Orpah) to remain in Moab, the land of their birth. Both originally decided to continue with Naomi (1:10–14). Yet, out of her concern, Naomi again entreated them to stay on in Moab. In verses 11–13, you can feel Naomi's helpless despair at having very little left to offer, as well as her confusion about God's hand in her life.

Finally, through tears, Orpah conceded to her mother-in-law's wishes and returned to Moab. Yet, Ruth was insistent, saying, "Entreat me not to leave you." Her oft-quoted poem of commitment is not mere emotion. She clearly is reaching beyond friendship to faith. By saying, "The LORD do so" it seems Ruth understood the nature of Yahweh. She invoked His name with an oath. Her commitment was rooted in an understanding of the living God, of whom she had learned primarily from Naomi. Although Ruth knew she would likely face prejudice in Judah as a Moabitess and might never remarry for the same reason, she remained loyal to Naomi and faithful to what she felt was right.

Ruth had to make a conscious, willful (v. 18, "determined," or "steadfastly minded") decision about her future. She could have remained in a place of comfort and familiarity, but she was unwilling to compromise her loyalty to Naomi or her faith in God. So, refusing to allow fear to rule her, she pressed ahead into the new place God had for her.

Read Luke 9:62; Philippians 3:12–15.

Questions:

Why do you believe the type of selfless loyalty Ruth displayed is a nearly forgotten concept in today's culture?

_____

_____

_____

Considering Jesus' words in Luke 9:62, in what way did Ruth live out the heart of this passage?

_____

_____

_____

Ruth made the difficult decision to press on though turning back would have been easier. What can you learn from her actions that can enable you to increase your ability to operate with loyal, determined faith?

✎ _____

_____

_____

Take a look at your own walk of faith. Are you more likely to press on through the rough times or do comfort and familiarity draw you away? Explain.

✎ _____

_____

_____

What place do choice and determination have in your ability to remain faithful and loyal in the face of daunting situations?

✎ _____

_____

_____

What steps can you take to increase your ability in these areas?

✎ _____

_____

_____

Probing the Depths

Pause to reflect and prayerfully allow the Holy Spirit to reveal any areas in your life where He would desire to "move you on." What would He ask you to leave behind or let go of from your past in order to reach unhindered toward His fullest purposes ahead? Where would the Lord desire to bring forgiveness or redemption in order to free you to embrace fully His complete plan? It is easy to get caught in the mire of "what if I'd done this, not gone there, or developed this talent?" But remember that the Lord forgives you and your past when you give it to Him (1 John 1:9). He doesn't even remember it anymore (Jeremiah 31:34)—why should you? Write down what the Holy Spirit is showing you about moving forward in your life.

Kingdom Life—*Faithfulness Brings Reward*

Read the second chapter of Ruth.

In this portion of the story, we see Ruth as a woman of action. In considering her plight with Naomi, who was too old to work, Ruth again made the decision to lay down her own comforts and desires to do what needed to be done.

The season was late summer, the temperature hot, the air was dry and dusty, and the constant bending, lifting, and hauling was back-breakingly difficult. Notice how Ruth was not necessarily an extraordinary gleaner or a shrewd businesswoman. She did not go to the fields and demand the rights that were hers as a widow. She simply began to work as best she knew how out of a willing heart. She simply trusted God with the results of her labor. And God took her offering of service and gave her favor and multiplied the fruit of her efforts, eventually bringing into her life Boaz, her kinsman-redeemer.

Ruth 2:3 says, "And she happened to come to the part of the field belonging to Boaz." In other words, she was led directly to the place where her redemption could be fulfilled. This has much to communicate to us about finding God's will, choosing God's way over your own, and your faithfulness to fulfill the daily duties of life. Ruth's willingness to humble herself and remain faithful to the menial (but necessary) tasks at hand put her in a position to meet her destiny!

Read Psalm 31:23; 101:6; Matthew 24:45–47; 25:21.

Questions:

How does God feel about faithfulness?

✎ _____

_____

What are the fruits of faithfulness?

✎ _____

_____

_____

How can pride negate faithfulness?

✎ _____

_____

_____

What is the prevailing attitude of a faithful heart?

✎ _____

_____

What are the resulting actions of a faithful heart?

✎ _____

_____

_____

Is pride or faithfulness the ruling factor in your decisions regarding service? Why do you believe this to be so? How can you increase your ability to walk in faithful service?

✎ _____

_____

_____

Kingdom Extra

Remaining faithful to the work God puts before us can be a challenge to our flesh. We may become tired or discouraged. But the Lord understands that and He will meet us with the perfect solution at the perfect time. We only need continue in faithful service. As we depend upon Him, have faith in His Word, pray for direction and blessing, and are motivated by our love for Christ, even common actions become fruitful and simple deeds holy!

Read 1 Corinthians 10:31; 15:58; 2 Thessalonians 3:6–13; Galatians 6:6–9.

Questions:

What do you believe it means to "do all to the glory of God"?

_____

_____

In the passage from 2 Thessalonians, what seems to be the heart attitude of those Paul addresses?

_____

_____

How can lack of faithfulness result in living in "a disorderly manner"?

_____

_____

In your own words, what benefits are reaped by the faithful?

_____

_____

_____

_____

Record Your Thoughts

Take a few minutes and consider some of the less-than-glamorous responsibilities that are yours to fulfill: housework, an unfulfilling place of employment, parenting (sometimes it can be difficult, draining, and discouraging). Maybe you find it taxing to open your home in hospitality or to discipline yourself in daily devotions. All these require discipline and faithfulness, yet don't always show immediate fruit. As you prayerfully examine your own life, list some areas where you'd like to grow in faithfulness or feel weary of the task at hand. Then reevaluate your heart attitude toward the day-to-day responsibilities that are yours to fulfill. Write down the thoughts and feelings that the Holy Spirit brings to light.

Just examining your life and realizing truth is not always enough. Our life with God is a partnership. He is a gentleman and shows no partiality (Acts 10:34), so He will never force change upon us without an act of our will being involved. Thus it is essential that we *ask* of God those things that we desire of Him. Review your writings above, then lift those things to God in prayer. Be specific in what you desire from the Lord. If you want forgiveness for imperfect attitudes, confess that now to Jesus. If you need His refreshing touch to bring new life to the mundane, ask Him. If you desire Him to multiply your efforts, tell Him. We *can* be faithful, because *He* is faithful to enable us! Hallelujah!

SESSION EIGHT

Ruth, Daughter of Redemption

 Kingdom Key—*God Is Faithful*

Psalm 17:8 Keep me as the apple of Your eye; hide me under the shadow of Your wings.

Ruth understood that though the realities of life can sometimes be harsh, seemingly unfair, or difficult to understand, there is a place of security, comfort, peace, and love: in the shadow of the wings of Almighty God—abiding in His presence. Herein lies the source of Ruth's strength, hope, and trust in God. Ruth's trusting response to God and her faithfulness throughout her circumstances allowed God's will to be released in and through her life. Ruth became a channel for His redemption.

We learned in the previous session how God views our faithfulness to the responsibilities of life, however large or seemingly insignificant they may seem. We saw that He honors and blesses the faithful, and intercepts us with His plan in the midst of our being diligent. Also realized was the importance of abiding in the Lord's presence, in order to find the strength to remain faithful.

Read Ruth 2 in preparation for this session. Also read Psalm 62: 1, 2, 5–8; 91:1–16.

Questions:

What does it mean to take refuge in the Lord?

_____

_____

In what ways should your expectations be "from" God?

_____

_____

In your own words, how does abiding (dwelling) in God's presence and taking refuge in Him lead to a faithful kingdom life?

_____

_____

_____

In reading these two Psalms passages, in what ways do you see the concept of diligence implied?

_____

_____

_____

How can you fit intentional times of refuge into your current lifestyle?

_____

_____

_____

What are some realistic goals you can set for yourself to set aside time to abide faithfully in His strengthening presence?

_____

_____

Word Wealth—*Apple*

Apple, *bath* (bath); Strong's #1323, and *iyshown* (ee-shone'); Strong's #380: *Bath* is a Hebrew word meaning daughter, apple, branch (this word is translated as "daughter" eight times in the Book of Ruth). *Bath* has at its root the word *banah*, which means to build, obtain children, or repair. The Hebrew word *iyshown* means pupil or that part of the eye through which light enters and sight is enabled. The picture this verse can create is one in which a daughter's heart cries out to God to be fully seen, fully known, and tenderly molded with His healing, upbuilding love.

Kingdom Life—*Diligence Pays*

The law of the ancient times in which Ruth lived required that famers leave the corners of their fields unharvested, and they were prohibited from gathering up the gleanings (what fell to the ground during harvest). These were to be left for the poor or a traveling stranger.

Ruth faithfully gleaned what she could from the fields to feed herself and her mother-in-law. She did not balk at hard work; nor did she wither into depression over their sad situation. Ruth was faithful in her tasks; she did not complain, she simply did what was before her to do and hoped for a better tomorrow.

Ruth did not have to wait long for a light to begin shining on her dark days. She "happened" to find the fields of Boaz and began her daily task of gleaning. However, what was apparent happenstance was actually the providence of divine sovereignty working on Ruth's behalf. Her seemingly random choice of Boaz's field was a path toward provision and appointed blessing—God's purpose being advanced in her life.

Read Psalm 139:13–16; Romans 8:28–30; Ephesians 2:10.

Questions:

Do you believe the circumstances of our lives are without design or that they are planned by God for our good? Why do you believe this? What is the biblical basis of your belief?

✎ _____

_____

_____

What other examples can you think of from Scripture that show divine providence at work in the lives of believers?

✎ _____

_____

_____

_____

In what ways can the passages above and your own discoveries in Scripture strengthen your resolve to trust as you diligently and faithfully apply yourself to the task at hand?

✎ _____

_____

_____

Behind the Scenes

Naomi was related to Boaz (whose name means "Swiftness") through her late husband, Elimelech. We are told Boaz was "a man of great wealth" (Ruth 2:1). In the original Hebrew text, this phrase encompasses more than economic prosperity. It reflects the possessor's power and social standing in the community.

Boaz presents one of the most dramatic figures found anywhere in the Old Testament to foreshadow the redeeming work of Jesus Christ. The role of the kinsman-redeemer, so beautifully fulfilled in Boaz's actions bringing about Ruth's personal restoration (which can be read in Ruth 4), speaks eloquently in this regard. His actions accomplish her inclusion in the blessings of Israel and bring her into the family line of the Messiah (Ephesians 2:19).

Kingdom Life—*Finding Favor*

Ruth had two disadvantages beyond her obvious poverty: she lived at a time when men would have very little to do with women in public; she was also a foreigner, who would normally be looked down upon in Judah. Yet she found favor in Boaz's eyes. To what can we attribute Boaz's amazing response? As Ruth put it in 2:10, "Why have I found favor in your eyes?"

There were many character traits displayed by Ruth that could have played a part in endearing her so quickly to Boaz. Read Ruth 2:7, 9, 10, 12, 17, 18, and 23, paying close attention to the qualities these verses reveal about Ruth.

Boaz was kind and comforting to Ruth and went out of his way to see that her needs were met. Ruth's response to such overt displays of generosity shows much about her. She did not stiffen her neck with pride and refuse his help; she was not suspicious of his motives; she was not resentful of his plenty in the face of her want; she did not put on a show of dejected misery and claim herself unworthy of Boaz's help.

In Ruth's response, we see her willingness to admit her need; we see an example of humility that opened the door to provision. We see in her the willingness to trust and a total lack of self-centered resentment for her needy state.

Read Matthew 5:3–10.

Questions:

Examine Ruth's responses and attitude in light of Jesus' words in Matthew 5:3–10. In what ways do you see the qualities Jesus promotes alive in Ruth?

_____

_____

_____

What steps can you take to make these same qualities more prevalent in your own life?

_____

_____

_____

What do you believe Jesus means when He says, "Blessed are" the ones who do as He teaches?

_____

_____

What place do you believe these attitudes and responses to the Lord have in the life of one who would minister in His name?

_____

_____

_____

Probing the Depths

In the story of Ruth and Boaz, we find a magnificent silhouette of the Master, foreshadowing His redemptive grace centuries in advance. As our "kinsman," He became flesh and came to earth as a man (John 1:14; Philippians 2:5–8). By His willingness to identify with the human family (we will see later how Boaz assumed the duties of his human family), Christ has worked a complete redemption of our plight. Further, Ruth's inability to do anything to alter her estate typifies absolute human helplessness (Romans 5:6); and Boaz's willingness to pay the complete price (Ruth 4:9) foreshadows Christ's full payment for our salvation (1 Corinthians 6:20; Galatians 3:13; 1 Peter 1:18, 19).

 ## Kingdom Life—*Know the Kinsman-Redeemer*

Read chapter 3 of Ruth.

In Ruth 3:2, Naomi refers to Boaz as a "relative." That one word is central to the theme and message of the Book of Ruth. Our language has no equivalent as the concept this term contains is related to the cultural obligation of a family member whose kinfolk have suffered loss. It involved the capacity of one relative to redeem a family member from slavery or to recoup property lost by reason of indebtedness. The expression "kinsman-redeemer" is often used in place of "relative" here in an attempt to express in English the combination of a human relationship with a divinely appointed role of recoverer.

The law (known as the Levirate law) regarding the preservation of families (Leviticus 25:25, 47–55) stated that a brother-in-law (Hebrew *levir*) could be called upon by a widow to act as her husband and raise up a son to carry on the name of the deceased. In Ruth's case, because there were no brothers-in-law, the nearest relative could take on that role. He was also required to "redeem" her, or to buy back the land a woman was forced to sell when she became a widow. Hence, the term "kinsman-redeemer" encompasses the widow's full redemption to her original status.

Read Isaiah 43:1; 47:4; 54:5; Revelation 5:9; Romans 8:29.

Questions:

What does it mean to you that Jesus is your Elder Brother?

_____

In what ways was Jesus' sacrifice on your behalf a mirror of the ancient Levirate law?

✎ _____

_____

_____

Consider all that Boaz brought into Ruth's life. In your own words, what is a redeemer?

✎ _____

_____

_____

With that list in mind, what has Christ provided for you?

✎ _____

_____

_____

The Levirate law encompassed restoration for the widow. What exactly is the restoration Jesus brings as our Kinsman-Redeemer?

✎ _____

_____

_____

How can continual realization of Christ's provision in your life allow you to more fully and effectively live out your faith with power and true commitment?

✎ _____

_____

_____

Behind the Scenes

The third chapter of Ruth begins with Naomi's advice to Ruth for securing Boaz's commitment as stipulated in Levirate law. Naomi's plan was bold but tender. Her direction and Ruth's ensuing action may appear to be seductive and inconsistent with the spiritual nobility of the book. To the contrary, however, Boaz's words, "You are a virtuous woman" (3:11), make clear that he believed her to be highly moral.

It is likely Naomi chose this exact time because it was nearing the end of harvest. Naomi may have feared Boaz would return to Bethlehem (his home) and the opportunity for Ruth to become his wife might come to nothing. Ruth, as a Moabitess, was probably not fully versed in Israelite law regarding a kinsman, so she was wisely open to the counsel of the authority God had placed in her life.

Word Wealth—*Virtuous*

Virtuous, *chayil* (khah'-yil); Strong's #2428: A force; capable, strong; with valor, excellence, substance, might. "Virtuous" implies more than doing well; there is a strength and courage in spite of difficulties. It comes from the root word *chiyl*, which includes trust and patient waiting in its definition. "Virtuous," then, is very close to "meek"—a quality of power and strength tempered by trusting patience.

Kingdom Life—*Above Reproach*

Ruth 3:6–8 tells of what initially took place when Ruth visited Boaz. She "uncovered his feet," but this should not be understood as overly forward or suggestive action. The obvious purpose was that the chill of the night would naturally awaken him in time and occasion his discovering her at his feet.

In verse 9, Ruth asks that Boaz take her under his wing. The literal translation here is "Spread the corner of your garment over your maidservant." This is the most tender point of the account, and the most liable to be misunderstood. The culture of the ancient Middle Eastern world embraced the practice of casting a garment over one being claimed for marriage (Ezekiel 16:8), a tradition to which Ruth clearly refers. It does not imply anything so inappropriate as a midnight tryst. Ruth was simply communicating, "Since you are my nearest relative, I ask that you take me as your wife."

Read Proverbs 31:10–31; Matthew 5:14–16; 1 Peter 2:11, 12.

Questions:

What qualities or attitudes would you attribute to the Proverbs 31 woman in light of her actions?

What are the results of a life lived virtuously before others?

Do you see "virtuous" as a descriptor of yourself? Why or why not?

Based on what we have learned this far in this study, what do you believe to be the source and empowerment of a virtuous life?

How can you become more connected to this Source?

_____

_____

_____

Record Your Thoughts

Boaz seized the opportunity to step in as kinsman-redeemer. Ruth became his wife and was not only redeemed, loved, and provided for, but was given a son, Obed, a forefather in the lineage of the Messiah. Ruth was privileged with the exceptional honor of becoming a mother in the line of our ultimate Redeemer, Jesus Christ!

The Old Testament contains many instances that are seen as a type, or a foreshadowing, of Jesus and His plan of redemption for mankind. But none are quite as tender and specific as the one found in Ruth, where Boaz so beautifully typifies the redeeming role of our Kinsman-Redeemer, the Lord Jesus Christ.

The Book of Ruth is a beautiful story of faithfulness and redemption, and models to women what to strive for in order to receive the Lord's restoration in their own lives:

1. To humbly continue in obedient and faithful service to all He calls you to.
2. To receive strength, security, and hope by daily abiding in the covering presence of the Almighty God.
3. To receive with gratitude the full redemption of all that's been lost from the hand of our Kinsman-Redeemer, the Lord Jesus Christ, whose greatest desire is to see you restored to wholeness, regardless of your background or past.

What are some further conclusions you may have reached from this study of the Book of Ruth?

_____

_____

_____

What impact has this session had on your understanding of the term "redeemed?" How can that insight help you be more committed and virtuous in your walk with the Lord?

✎ _____

_____

_____

SESSION NINE

Esther, Daughter of Purpose

 Kingdom Key—*God Has a Plan*

Romans 8:28 And we know that all things work together for good to those who love God, to those who are the called according to His purpose.

The Greek word translated in Romans 8:28 as "purpose" is the Greek word *prothesis* (proth'-es-is). This word suggests the setting forth of a definite, deliberate plan. A *prothesis* is a proposition, an advance plan, an intention, and/or a design (Strong's #4286).

God is at work to cause events and circumstances to ultimately conclude for the good of His people. And often He uses us, His people, as agents in that process, making us part of His advance plan, fulfilling His purpose through our lives. The question is not whether God will work in our lives; the question is how we will respond as He does. Our reaction to God's working in our lives is as varied as the people within whom He works; and the types of situations He brings about to work His will into our lives and our world are seemingly without limit.

Read Jeremiah 29:11; Romans 5:1–5; Philippians 4:8.

Questions:

What attitude will allow us to face difficulties in life with the confidence that God has a plan?

Go back and read Psalm 42. With this psalm in mind, along with the verses listed above, what is a healthy, productive response to times of trouble?

_____

_____

_____

What is God's prime objective in working in and through our lives?

_____

_____

_____

How would keeping this fact in mind allow you to line up more quickly and easily with God's work in your life?

_____

_____

_____

Kingdom Life—*Connected and Confident*

First, read the entire Book of Esther for an overview of her life. It's barely ten chapters, but it holds some incredible kingdom insights.

Esther apparently understood the core truth of Romans 8:28, though it would be centuries before Paul penned the words. Esther allowed herself to be used mightily of God for the purpose of saving her people, the Jews, from destruction. She operated in full trust of God and lived up to her commitment to Him by obediently placing her life in His hands. Esther was connected at the heart to the truth of God and remained confident of His intentions and His ways. Her commitment was such that she willingly risked everything to be of service to Him.

It is interesting to note the name of God does not appear even once in the book (this is also true in the Song of Solomon); but also note how His whispered presence and wise ways are constantly at work behind the scenes.

Read Psalm 25:1–5; 31:1–5; 61:1–4.

Questions:

What do you believe is the motivation of a life that is connected to and confident in God?

How can trust in God grow in the heart of a believer? What Scripture passages can you find that support your answer?

What is the core reason for trusting God?

In reviewing your walk with the Lord to this point, what observations can be made of your trust in God?

With the verses from Psalms listed above in mind, what steps can you take to increase your ability to connect to and be confident in God?

_____

_____

 Behind the Scenes

The Book of Esther takes its name from the beautiful, orphaned Jewess who became the queen of the Persian king, Ahasuerus. He is generally believed to have been King Xerxes I who succeeded Darius I in 485 B.C. He ruled for twenty years over 127 provinces from India to Ethiopia. Ahasuerus lived in the Persian capital of Shushan. During his reign, a number of Jews were still in Babylon under Persian rule, even though they had been free to return to Jerusalem (Ezra 1; 2) for over fifty years. The story takes place over a period of four years, starting in the third year of Ahasuerus' reign.

King Ahasuerus was one of the mightiest rulers of all time. His empire had become the largest and wealthiest known to man. Raised in this atmosphere, Ahasuerus was a man accustomed to tremendous wealth and power and would not be questioned or crossed.

 Kingdom Life—*Display True Beauty*

In chapter one of Esther, we meet King Ahasuerus and Queen Vashti. We are told Queen Vashti was "beautiful to behold" (1:11). The king was hosting a special feast; because of her beauty, he wished to show Vashti off to his guests. But Vashti refused. The drunkenness and debauchery that characterized the Persian feasts may well have been the reason. Yet Vashti's refusal put her in a precarious position. She was not just refusing her husband; she had chosen to deny the king. Some might applaud her as a courageous woman with her own mind. Others might feel it was within her right to refuse her husband's request. Still others might be appalled at her contempt for the king's request. Regardless of your own reaction, Vashti stood her ground and not only refused one of the king's summons, but she twice refused his invitation. For her refusal, she was denied access to the king forever after.

What took place in 2:8–16 was akin to an ancient beauty pageant! The kingdom was searched for the most beautiful of virgins, one of whom would replace Queen Vashti. Beautiful young women from all over the kingdom were prepared and brought before the king.

Where Vashti had been "beautiful to behold," Esther was "lovely and beautiful" (2:7) outside; but there was something much greater than a pleasing face to Esther's beauty. We are told she "pleased" the king (2:9), but she also "obtained [the] favor" (2:15) of everyone she met. Esther 2:15 also shows the astute wisdom balanced with the gracious humility that Esther possessed.

Read Esther 2:9, 10, 15, 17, 20; 4:4, 5, 16; 7:2–4; 8:3.

Questions:

Combining all the information contained in the verses cited above, what characteristics would you ascribe to Esther?

✎ _____

_____

_____

In what ways do Esther's characteristics and those displayed by Vashti differ? What do you believe was the core reason for the differences?

✎ _____

_____

_____

Being completely transparent, which of the traits of Esther do you possess? Which of the traits of Vashti do you possess?

✎ _____

_____

_____

With this in mind, what can you learn from Esther's attitude and choices?

_____

_____

_____

Word Wealth—*Beautiful*

Beautiful, *towb* (tobe); Strong's #2896: Good, beautiful, best, bountiful, cheerful, glad, gracious, kind, loving, pleasant, precious, ready, sweet. *Towb* is a much broader, encompassing definition of beauty than simply a comment about pleasing physical features.

Kingdom Life—*Obey the Governing Authorities*

The differences between Esther and Vashti went beyond demeanor and personality. The attitudes of their hearts were even more dissimilar.

In Vashti's refusal of the king's summons, she displayed a rebellious, self-willed attitude. Though we cannot know all the dynamics involved, we can definitely understand her refusal to have been out of order and in direct defiance to the authority of the king.

Esther, on the other hand, displayed a humble heart and an understanding of submission to authority. She seemed to realize that submission is not demeaning, but empowering. Those who operate under the authority in their lives enjoy the protection of that authority and the benefits of humble submission.

Read 1 Corinthians 5:6; Hebrews 12:15; Psalm 10:17; 18:27; 25:9; 149:4; Proverbs 3:34; 11:2; Isaiah 29:19.

Questions:

Do you believe it is ever the right course of action to disobey authority? In what situations is disobedience acceptable and what is the biblical basis for your belief?

✎ _____

_____

_____

What five words describe your current attitude toward and/or response to authority in your life? What can you conclude about yourself from this?

✎ _____

_____

_____

What are the traits displayed in the life of one who is truly humble?

✎ _____

_____

_____

What do you understand as the connection between humility and submission to authority?

✎ _____

_____

_____

Why do you believe humility is upheld in Scripture as a trait that releases God's mercy and help?

✎ _____

_____

_____

Kingdom Life—*Seek Wisdom*

Esther's relationship with Mordecai was one of mutual respect. Mordecai trusted Esther; and she, in turn, trusted the counsel of the one who had raised her. This relationship, empowered by a strong faith in the Lord, had built within Esther a confidence and a proper view of authority figures. Being in right relationship to God and those He had placed in her life had also freed Esther to become a strong, poised woman of God—a woman ready to face the challenges of life head on. Esther 2:17, 18 points to the qualities in Esther's life that were evident even to the king. Because she was raised in the home of the devout Israelite, Mordecai, the difference of her godly and gracious manner was likely magnified in the presence of the idolatrous Persian women.

Read Exodus 18:19–24; 1 Kings 12:8–16; Proverbs 1:5; 11:14; 19:20.

Questions:

Why do you believe Scripture exhorts us to seek out counsel from others?

With the passages above in mind, what do you believe can be gained from "a multitude of counselors"?

Who are the people in your own life from whom you receive wisdom and insight to further your own walk with the Lord?

What qualities do those people possess that drew you and caused you to trust their input into your life?

✎ _____

_____

_____

_____

What steps can you take to see those qualities growing in your own life?

✎ _____

_____

_____

_____

Kingdom Extra

A practical way to live by the counsel of the wise is to be prepared in advance. Sit down with your spouse, parents, or those you are most closely associated with and compose a list of those believers in Christ from whom you would most readily receive counsel (your "counsel council"!). The list can include your pastor, elders, friends, family, financial advisors, and so on. Make them aware that you look to them for leadership. Pray for them regularly. Then when a challenge or crisis presents itself, you are not scrambling to figure out what to do, but ready with a "multitude of counselors [for] safety" (Proverbs 11:14).

Behind the Scenes

Haman is the villain of this story. He was an Amalekite and a descendant of Agag, the ruler who was spared by Saul in disobedience to God (1 Samuel 15). The Amalekites had long been enemies of Israel, even attacking them during their journey to the Promised Land (Exodus 17:8–14; Deuteronomy 25:17–19). Haman hated the Jews and sought to rid the country of their presence. But Haman did not know Esther was a Jew.

Haman's hatred stemmed from an inbred prejudice against the Jewish people. When Mordecai (Esther's cousin) refused to bow in reverence to Haman, the hatred grew into an unquenchable thirst for vengeance. But Haman was not content to seek revenge on only Mordecai; his hatred exploded into a desire to see all Jews exterminated.

Much to the shame and disgrace of the human condition, the ugly face of prejudice is not only found in biblical stories of long ago. Prejudice can be found throughout history and is much too alive and well in our world today. As with Haman, prejudice is most often a result of generational lies—untrue beliefs that are passed from top to bottom of a family tree or from age to age throughout a culture. When this inbred prejudice takes root in a heart, any wrong or slight (real or imagined) attributed to the maligned peoples adds fuel to a destructive inferno.

Hatred in any form is a ravenous condition. It continually seeks reason to build itself up and fortify its reserves. Hatred is a powerful weapon in our enemy's arsenal; hatred bears the mark of the one who seeks to destroy all that God loves. Remember the words of 1 Peter 5:8, "Be sober, be vigilant; because your adversary the devil walks about like a roaring lion, seeking whom he may devour." When hatred fuels our attitudes and actions, we align ourselves with our enemy. Prejudice is hatred in one of its most disastrous, insidious forms. Those who serve the Lord should never enter in to this alliance with Satan.

 Kingdom Life—*Rise to Meet Your Destiny*

Esther was a Jewish orphan—a virtual nonentity, raised by her cousin. Based on her circumstances, Esther's life held no particular promise. But her story shows us clearly that God will open destiny to any person who will keep His priorities. Even in the presence of acceptance, acclaim, and recognition (huge issues in the heart of an orphan), success, wealth, and luxury, Esther retained her sense of perspective and integrity.

Esther's Hebrew name, Hadassah, means "Myrtle." It refers to the well-known and beautiful evergreen shrub. Esther reflected the qualities of the myrtle shrub in her courage and obedience. These traits clearly did not wither, even when she faced death. In Persian, "Esther" means "Star." Again, this name is descriptive of the woman to whom it belonged—Esther's beauty, grace, and character shown bright and unwavering against the darkness threatening the Jewish people.

In this incredible woman's life, we find a faithfulness that can call us deeper into the things of God's kingdom. We find a security in God and commitment to His purposes that can provoke our own faith. We see in Esther a respect for the power of prayer; she recognized the reality of the spiritual realm and the Holy Spirit's resources. Her unswerving will to lay down her own life for others is an example of kingdom life at its finest. Her practical good sense and patience in pursuing her enterprise are wisdom in action. Esther's life spoke loudly to the people of her day. It can speak just as loudly to us.

The power of God on behalf of His people was evident even to the wicked of Esther's day. The Jews often faced perilous times, as we do today. The temptation is to recoil in fear and to wish you had been born at another time or lived in another place. But God, in His wisdom, has given you to the kingdom for this very time. You need not fear, for He will keep you, sustain you, and fulfill His purpose through you. You only need walk as Esther walked—in obedience and faithful commitment before Him.

Read Matthew 6:1–6; Luke 12:22–34; James 4:1–10.

Questions:

What heart attitude do you believe was at the core of Esther's faithful commitment to the Lord and her people?

✎ _____

_____

_____

God showered Esther with His favor. What does God's favor mean to you?

✎ _____

_____

_____

What do you believe results in the flow of God's favor into a life?

_____

_____

_____

Based on the story of Esther, what do you believe to be the purpose of God's favor?

_____

_____

_____

What steps can you take to be a recipient of God's favor?

_____

_____

_____

Probing the Depths

Read chapters 4 through 10 once again.

When Mordecai called upon Esther to take news of the Jews' plight to the king, she could have taken the easy way, the wide road (Matthew 7:13, 14). Even though the hateful decree from Haman could have meant her death, she could have finessed and charmed her way into a place of personal safety through the king's favor (5:3, 6). Had she chosen the easier path, she would have thwarted the purpose of God for her own life through selfish ambition or outright disobedience to what she knew was right. But she heeded the profound voice of Mordecai. She laid aside her own dreams and desires and came to the aid of God's people. She demonstrated her firm faith in the mercy and providence of God.

Esther realized her life had far greater purpose than merely maintaining her own immediate comfort and status quo. Because her heart was tender, Mordecai's words pierced it through; she committed herself to putting her life on the line to save others. Esther's heart was turned from her own self-interests to the plans and purposes of God.

Ultimately, the king not only welcomed the uninvited Esther into his presence, but later offered her corulership with himself (5:3). Later, he awarded her the right to use his signet ring (8:8), the symbol of his authority. This gesture solidified a new level of authority in Esther's life. Her courage resulted in great deliverance of God's people.

Truly effective women are those who turn from their own short-sighted agenda to God's eternal purpose.

Record Your Thoughts

It was in losing her life that Esther actually found her purpose. Read Matthew 16:25. The temptation is to think, "If only my life could be spent in such grand significance, as was Esther's." But the truth is that, at every turn, there are opportunities to deny ourselves (lose our lives) for the sake of others. Only God Himself knows the eternal value of laying down your life to support your husband, raise a child, teach a Sunday school class, or witness to a neighbor. The point is to serve Him to your utmost where He has placed you, and that preparation will lead to a broader influence if such is His desire for you. God has given you to His kingdom for *today*. Let that be what guides your every deed, and you cannot help but fulfill His purpose for you.

What aspect of Esther's life has most impacted you as you worked your way through this lesson?

✎ _____

_____

_____

What resolves have you been led to make as a result of a deeper understanding of Esther's heart and motivations?

✎ _____

_____

_____

What practical steps can you take to place yourself within the flow of God's blessing and impact your world for Him?

✎ _____

_____

_____

SESSION TEN

Mary, Daughter and Mother

 Kingdom Key—*Trust*

John 2:5 Whatever He says to you, do it.

Through the ages, there have been women who have represented the ideals to which we all should aspire. But none have had as profound or eternal an impact as a modest Jewish maid, who bore from her body the Redeemer of the world.

Mary responded to the call of God on her life with the words, "Behold the maidservant of the Lord! Let it be to me according to your word" (Luke 1:38). Within these simple words lies a submission and trust more rare than gold and much more costly. Mary simply trusted and believed in God and acted accordingly. Nothing could dissuade her from her purpose; nothing could make her doubt. She heard from God and stood firm on the revelation she received from Him.

Mary was the first to believe on Christ as Savior and Redeemer. She was the first to place her trust in Him. Even as she held His lifeless body following His crucifixion, she knew He had given her a life that would never end.

Read Psalm 18:30; 37:5; 62:5–8; Proverbs 30:5; Isaiah 26:3; 50:10.

Questions:

In your opinion, how are faith and trust connected?

✎ _____

_____

If you were completely and utterly convinced of God's love and faithfulness, what difference would this confidence make in your daily life? What difference would this confidence make in your ministry to the body of Christ?

✎ _____

_____

_____

In what ways do you find it difficult to trust God? Why do you believe this is so?

✎ _____

_____

_____

According to the passages above, what awaits those who trust in God?

✎ _____

_____

_____

What other passages of Scripture can you find that give further insight into the benefits of trusting God?

✎ _____

_____

_____

How do you fare in your daily life in living out Mary's directive in John 2:5?

_____

_____

_____

_____

Kingdom Life—*Godly Motherhood*

To prepare for this session, read Luke 1:26–56.

Mary was a mother among mothers. She, as well as many other women in the Bible, models to us the great privilege and high calling of the unique gift of God to women alone—motherhood.

Even if you have no children of your own, there is much to be gleaned from a closer look at the mothers of the Bible. Among the many principles found, there are three that can readily be seen. First, to understand the comfort of a mother's love is to know more fully the tender heart of God (Isaiah 66:13). Second, to give that love away to another, particularly children you may know or be related to, is much needed and welcomed. And third, to share what you have learned with a young, desperate mother could be a help beyond measure.

Mary was truly a role model in her humility, obedience, fidelity, and devotion as a woman, wife, and mother. However, this study will focus on the nine key elements we see in Mary's example of godly motherhood. It is apparent she understood the priority of knowing God and His ways, and she put Him above all other desires in her life. It was from that same rich well of relationship that she drew the wisdom and grace to nurture Jesus and her other children in the ways of the Lord.

The most lasting gift a mother can give her children is to live according to God's order: to first love the Lord with all her heart (Deuteronomy 10:12), love and honor her husband in the same fashion (Colossians 3:12–14; Ephesians 5:33), *then* love and cherish her children (Titus 2:4). When those priorities are confused, there can be sorrowful consequences.

Read Proverbs 31:10–31.

Questions:

What qualities are displayed by the virtuous woman that allow her to display excellence as a mother?

_____

_____

_____

In what way would those same qualities enable a woman to walk faithfully with the Lord?

_____

_____

_____

In what way would those same qualities enable a woman to be an effective leader in the kingdom?

_____

_____

_____

Do you believe these qualities to be desirable for only women? Why or why not?

_____

_____

_____

Kingdom Extra

There is a wonder surrounding Mary, the mother of Jesus, which transcends traditional religious thought. That she was a privileged vessel, chosen to bear God's Son, is wonder enough, for she is a participant in the miracle of the Incarnation at a level no other human being can comprehend. It is clear that she did not claim to understand it herself, but simply worshiped God in humble acknowledgment of the phenomenon engulfing her existence: "My soul magnifies the Lord," she exclaims (Luke 1:46). We can hardly fathom the bewildering moments she experienced when Simeon prophesied future mental and emotional suffering (Luke 2:35). We can only imagine what feelings and thoughts she had when she and Joseph spoke with Jesus after they thought He was lost in Jerusalem (Luke 2:49, 50). It's hard to comprehend her feelings when Jesus gently rebuffed her at the wedding in Cana (John 2:4). And when Jesus seemed to reject her and the rest of His earthly family in Matthew 12:46–50, it must have taxed the understanding of her mother's heart.

Kingdom Life—*Wisdom's Focus*

Mary's experiences prompt our learning the wisdom of persistence and obedience in following God's basic directive on our lives, even when the details of the outworking of His plan are unclear and mystifying.

Mary is a study in the pathway forward in God's will. She could have sought an elevated position among those who recognized Jesus as the Messiah; but Mary did not promote herself. Instead, she remained steadfast with Him all the way to the cross—she did not seek to protect herself. After Jesus rose from death and returned to heaven, she obediently joined Jesus' faithful disciples in the upper room, waiting as He commanded for the coming of the Holy Spirit (Acts 1:14).

Mary is a model of responsive obedience. She lived out her own directive to the servants at Cana—timeless advice for all ages: "Whatever He [Jesus] says to you, do it" (John 2:5).

Read Psalm 111:10; 119:73–80, 101–105, 129–135; Proverbs 2:1–9; 3:5, 6.

Questions:

How can you know God's Word—His directive—for you at any and all points in your life?

In your opinion, what is at the heart of obedience to God? Give the scriptural basis for your answer.

How can you influence those around you by operating in obedience to God?

What promises can you find in the passages above that belong to those who will seek God's directive and obey His commands?

Kingdom Life—*The Privilege to Nurture*

All mothers (whether in the natural or in the spiritual realm) can consider themselves "highly favored." They are uniquely privileged with the high calling of bringing forth and nurturing life. Psalm 127:3 tells us that "children are a heritage," meaning *they belong to God*. He has a destiny and purpose for *each* of His children (Romans 8:28). Therefore, the privilege of motherhood rests not just in being instrumental in the process of bringing forth life. The true privilege comes from being entrusted with the faithful stewardship of the life-gifts of God—those who will one day act as His agents, both now and through eternity (Revelation 5:10; 22:5).

Read Proverbs 2:1–5; 22:6; Titus 2:1–5.

Questions:

In what ways are natural motherhood (raising and nurturing children) and spiritual motherhood (leading others to spiritual life and maturity) similar?

_____

_____

_____

What should be the focus of a natural or spiritual mother's heart?

_____

_____

_____

In what ways does an earthly family give us insight into God's heart?

_____

_____

_____

In what ways can the relationships within an earthly family prepare us to live fruitful lives in God's kingdom?

_____

_____

_____

Kingdom Extra

In Luke 1:29, 30, we see that Mary was troubled by what the angel said to her. To comfort her, the angel said, "Do not be afraid, Mary, for you have found favor with God."

Fear can totally derail our journey of faith. Fear paralyzes us and causes us to seek out the familiar. Fear keeps us from accepting new experiences from the hand of God. Fear keeps us rooted in what *was* and prevents us from discovering what *will be* if we but trust and follow God's directive in our lives.

Kingdom Life—*Embrace Purpose*

Read Luke 1:31—2:7.

You will note when the angel spoke to Mary, he was very clear regarding the purpose intended for Jesus. And God also has a clear purpose for your children (both natural and spiritual)—and for you as their mother and/or mentor.

The scene in 2:1–7 grabs at the heart of anyone who has ever loved a child. Joseph and Mary had traveled almost seventy miles in a most primitive fashion to a crowded city where the only resting place was a barn. It is here the Savior entered the world He was soon to redeem. The young parents wrapped Jesus in "swaddling cloths." This so tenderly depicts the primary purpose of parents. It is not to provide every luxury and comfort, but to "wrap" (cover, love, hold, protect) their children.

Throughout Scripture, God reveals Himself as a loving parent who is tender, close to His children, and sensitive to their needs—teaching, encouraging, helping, and healing them. Growing up is not something that He leaves to chance. He is a God who conscientiously *nurtures* His children. Likewise, God entrusts the young and immature to those who can feed into their lives, allowing His own nurturing heart to flow through them to those who are growing toward maturity.

Read Isaiah 49:10, 15, 16; Matthew 6:25–32.

Questions:

Why do you believe the passage in Isaiah uses feminine imagery to describe God's heart toward His people?

_____

_____

_____

In what ways have you experienced the tender nurturing of God?

_____

_____

_____

How does knowing God is a loving, nurturing parent affect your understanding of His call on your life?

_____

_____

_____

In what ways can you model this type of parental love to those in your life?

_____

_____

_____

Probing the Depths

Read Proverbs 22:6 again.

"Train up," as used in this verse, has the idea of a parent graciously investing in a child whatever wisdom, love, nurture, and discipline is needed for him to become fully committed to God. It presupposes the emotional and spiritual maturity of the parent to do so. To raise a child up "in the way he should go" is to train according to the unique personality, gifts, and aspirations of the child. It also means to train the child to avoid whatever natural tendencies he might have that would prevent total commitment to God (for example: a weak will, a lack of discipline, moodiness).

Throughout the Bible, the training of children often rested with the mother, as is still true today. This by no means precludes the importance of the father's involvement (Ephesians 6:4). But the reality is that the primary caregiver will have the most opportunity for influence, and that is usually the mother. Though this role is one that requires diligent commitment, the fruit of a mother's labor can have a profound impact. God has purposed many things for His daughters, but none as full of potential as the faithful nurturing and training of the next generation.

 ## Kingdom Life—*Empowered by the Spirit*

Turn to Luke 1 and read verses 34 and 35. Mary said to the angel, "How can this be?" Many who would raise up servants for our Master may ask themselves a similar question. "How can this be done? How can I shape a vessel that will be fit for the Master's use?"

It was the power of the Spirit of God that began the miracle in Mary's life. That same power is available to us today. Acts 1:8 tells us, "You shall receive power when the Holy Spirit has come upon you." The Holy Spirit is the Person and the Power by which assistance and ability are given for serving, for sharing the life and power of God's kingdom with others. This includes our natural and spiritual children. The Holy Spirit brings fruit into our lives that enables us to minister powerfully and effectively to those who look to us for nurturing.

Read Galatians 5:22, 23.

Questions:

God's Spirit makes available to us certain qualities that enable us to minister to others in truly loving, nurturing ways. In reading this list of nine qualities, which are dependent upon a personal choice?

✎ _____

_____

_____

God's Word refers to these qualities as "fruit." What truths can be gleaned from this analogy?

✎ _____

_____

_____

Which type of "fruit" causes the most struggle for you? Why do you believe this is so?

✎ _____

_____

_____

Drawing from the life of Mary, what attitude and actions can enable you to more readily display the qualities the Holy Spirit brings?

✎ _____

_____

_____

 Kingdom Life—*A True Disciple Is Obedient*

To be a faithful mother or mentor, one *must* be an obedient disciple. Only God knows His plans for His children; thus, it is essential that you follow His leading and directives for nurturing them. Because "children will do as you do, not as you say," what more loving example than to live before them a life of obedience to Christ (1 John 5:2)?

Mary called herself a "maidservant" of the Lord (Luke 1:38). To be a true disciple of Christ and to raise up other devoted disciples, obedience must be alive and well in a committed heart. Obedience is the response of faith to any instruction from God. Jesus taught that true faith will always be manifested in obedience to God's revealed will. Jesus came willingly, and though it cost Him everything, He was obedient to every purpose of God.

If we would be faithful servants of Christ and effective godly ministers to those placed in our care, we must adopt Mary's attitude—we must submit our plans and futures to God's will.

Read Matthew 20:25–28; Romans 11:29; Hebrews 13:5, 6.

Questions:

For what two reasons did Jesus come? In what ways should our lives of faith be impacted by this revelation?

_____

_____

_____

_____

The walk of faith is difficult; it is more so when nurturing others in the faith. Many times, progress will be slow in coming and setbacks in the lives of those you nurture may be many. How can you guard against becoming discouraged or discontent?

_____

_____

_____

_____

As a mother or mentor, there will be times when you will make mistakes and maybe even times you will unintentionally hurt those to whom you minister. What comfort can you find in Romans 11:29 that can help you through times of self-recrimination and self-doubt?

✎ _____

_____

_____

Record Your Thoughts

Finally, read Luke 1:45. Mary *believed* and trusted in the almighty power and faithfulness of God, enough so to spend her life in service and devotion to His kingdom (1:38). She did not feel burdened; she was not discontent in the difficult task to which she was called. Rather, her words to Elizabeth fairly vibrate with pure joy. Mary sang out her praise to God and "rejoiced in God" her Savior (v. 47). Her heart poured forth in a stream of worship and adoration.

As we close this session, let us read David's words of praise from Psalm 145:1–3: "I will extol You, my God, O King; and I will bless Your name forever and ever. Every day I will bless You, and I will praise Your name forever and ever. Great is the LORD, and greatly to be praised; and His greatness is unsearchable."

Such is the attitude of a faithful, obedient heart.

Are you often carried away in praise and thanksgiving to God? Why do you believe this is so?

✎ _____

_____

_____

How can a life of praise enable you to be a more effective nurturer in the kingdom of God?

✎ _____

_____

_____

What aspect of this session most impacted you? Why do you believe this is so? How will this affect your walk of faith in the future?

SESSION ELEVEN

Priscilla,
Daughter of Virtue

 Kingdom Key—*In His Image*

Genesis 1:27 So God created man in His own image; in the image of God He created him; male and female He created them.

God's heart to build a dwelling place for Himself in the earth is seen in His creation of man and woman—together, the foundation of the house of the Lord. Through the two of them together, He intended to live and reveal Himself in the world. Through them, God intended to manifest His character and authority (image), express His dominion over the earth, display His indisputable power over the works of darkness, and subdue His archenemy, Satan. The first man and woman were a microcosm of the church, signaling that God's glory would forever be seen in the earth through the combined expression of male and female. Now, as then, God's blessing—His promise of success—is upon our unity.

Read Genesis 1—2; Romans 8:29, 30; 1 Peter 3:7.

Questions:

What do you believe it means to have "dominion" over the earth?

✎ _____

_____

_____

What distinction in individual roles did God present to Adam and Eve prior to the fall?

What do you believe it means to be "conformed" to the image of Jesus?

Why do you think 1 Peter 3:7 refers to women as "the weaker vessel"?

What understanding can you gain from these passages as they apply to men and women acting as co-servants within the church?

Word Wealth—*Dominion*

Dominion, *moshel* (moh-shel'); Strong's #4915: Dominion, sovereignty, jurisdiction, rulership. This noun comes from the verb *mashal*, meaning to rule, govern, or reign. It signifies dominion or the exercise of authority. *Mashal* conveys the thought of a strong and sovereign ruling over one's subjects. The noun *moshel* refers to the realm of rulership (both geographical and governmental) that belongs to a sovereign authority.

Kingdom Life—*Called to Unity*

We have seen that God created the first couple in His image. He also called this first of all couples to be "one flesh" (Genesis 2:24). Their unity was to be absolutely complete. We can understand how profound this unity was intended to be by looking at the Hebrew word *echad*, which is translated as "one" in Genesis 2:24. This word means one, unit, or unity; it is the same word used to describe God in Deuteronomy 6:4: "The LORD our God, the LORD is one!"

It was not until the entrance of sin into the world that the absolute unity between Adam and Eve was broken (Genesis 3:12, 13). It was at this point that their relationship became contentious (Genesis 3:15, 16) and they took on separate identities (Genesis 3:20). The breach in their relationship was a direct result of sin.

However, Jesus came to set us free from the damaging influence of sin. Therefore, the breach in relationship between man and woman can and will be healed when the relationship is founded in the Lord and empowered by His love.

Read Acts 18:2–4, 18, 19, 24–26; Romans 16:3–5; 1 Corinthians 16:19; 2 Timothy 4:19.

Questions:

What can you glean from these passages regarding the relationship between Priscilla and Aquila?

_____

_____

In reading about Priscilla's life and ministry, what aspects of God's original plan for the relationship between men and women (husband and wife) do you see in operation?

_____

_____

In reviewing your own relationships with men (husband or others), what aspects of God's original plan do you see lacking?

_____

_____

_____

Being completely transparent, what part do your own attitudes play in this lack?

_____

_____

_____

Kingdom Life—*Strive for Excellence*

God determined that mankind (meaning the race, not specifying gender) was to have His very image and likeness. We are spiritual beings who possess a body, soul, and spirit. We possess intelligence, perception, and self-determination that far exceed that of any other earthly being.

These traits, together with mankind's prominence in the order of creation, imply intrinsic worth of each human individual.

We have been given capacity and ability; these constitute accountability and responsibility. We should never be pleased to dwell on a level of existence lower than that on which God has made it possible to dwell. We should strive to be the best we can be and to reach the highest levels we can reach. To do less is to be unfaithful stewards of the life entrusted to us.

Read Psalm 8:4, 5; 139:13, 14; Proverbs 31:10–31.

Questions:

What do you believe it means that God has "crowned" us with "glory and honor"?

✎ _____

_____

_____

What do you believe it means that we are "fearfully and wonderfully made"?

✎ _____

_____

_____

What impact should these two passages have on those with a tendency toward a negative self image?

✎ _____

_____

_____

What impact should these two passages have on those who believe women are less able to lead?

✎ _____

_____

_____

In what ways do you see the Proverbs 31 woman living a life with full knowledge of her God-given, intrinsic value?

✎ _____

_____

_____

Kingdom Extra

"Who can find a virtuous wife?" asks the writer of Proverbs 31. Proverbs 31:10–31 sets forth the high standard for womanhood, apparently drawn not by some romantic male, but by one who was herself a virtuous woman (Proverbs 31:1). This lesson will examine more closely the qualities of the virtuous woman (for it includes principles applicable to more than just wives) and how they were reflected in the lives of Priscilla and other wives of the Bible.

But while studying, keep in mind that the commandments of the Lord "are not burdensome" (1 John 5:3). Before being tempted to feel condemned or weighed down by the seemingly unattainable standards of Proverbs 31, understand that they are intended as inspiring goals. And, though *attainable*, they do require time, effort, prayer, and the working of God through grace to become fully operational in one's life. Remember, "I can do all things through Christ who strengthens me" (Philippians 4:13).

Kingdom Life—*Live in Unity*

Genesis 2:18 says, "And the Lord God said, 'It is not good that man should be alone; I will make him a helper comparable to him.'" The word "helper" indicates that Adam's strength for all he was called to be and do was inadequate in itself. Adam needed Eve; she brought to him those qualities and abilities necessary to be about the work of the Lord. The word "comparable" denotes Eve was created as a complement to Adam. Together they could live out their full potential as they were called to daily work, procreation, and mutual support through companionship.

Read 1 Corinthians 11:3–9; Ephesians 5:22–33.

Questions:

What is your initial reaction to the passages above? Is there a feeling of inferiority engendered by these verses? What leads you to this reaction?

✎ _____

_____

_____

_____

What is your reaction to the fact that women are called to submit to their husbands? Why do you believe this is so?

✎ _____

_____

_____

_____

Do you believe submission to be a limiting factor for women? In what way?

✎ _____

_____

_____

_____

What is your personal "doctrine" of submission? What is your biblical basis for these beliefs?

✎ _____

_____

_____

_____

_____

Taking these passages in conjunction with your study thus far, what do you believe to be a balanced and healthy view of these passages specifically and submission in general?

_____

_____

_____

Probing the Depths

Reread 1 Corinthians 11:3. The relationship between God as "Head" and Christ as Son is given as a model for the relationship between husband and wife. When the Bible reveals how the Father and the Son relate to each other, it also tells us something about the way that husbands and wives should relate to each other. Describe in your own words the dynamics of a marriage that follows the pattern set forth in the kingdom of God.

Look up the following passages and list all the marriage principles you can find within them that are illustrated through the relationship between Jesus and the Father: John 5:20, 22; 8:29, 49, 54; 10:17, 30; 11:42; 14:9, 11, 28, 31; 16:15.

Kingdom Life—Be Imitators of the Godly

Priscilla, wife of Aquila and minister of the gospel of Christ, will be held up as a model throughout the course of this session. You may want to reread the references to her in Scripture: Acts 18:2–4, 18, 19, 24–26; Romans 16:3–5; 1 Corinthians 16:19; 2 Timothy 4:19. As you read, make note of Priscilla's attitudes and actions, first as a woman, and then as a wife. You will note how Aquila and Priscilla are *always* listed together, never one without the other. This fact alone reveals much about their relationship. Priscilla and Aquila were joined in marriage and in ministry; they were unified in purpose and calling. They seemed to have lived out Jesus' words concerning marriage: "From the beginning of the creation, God made them male and female. For this reason a man shall leave his father and mother and be joined to his wife, and the two shall become one flesh; so then they are no longer two, but one flesh" (Mark 10:6-8).

Priscilla obviously understood "the way of God" (Acts 18:26) and could minister His truth effectively (1 Corinthians 16:19).

Read Proverbs 31:10–31 again.

Questions:

Take a moment and list things a godly wife can do or be that are of high value to her husband. Which of these qualities is most difficult for you to put into practice in your own life?

_____

_____

_____

_____

How can each of these qualities serve to make you a more effective servant-leader in the kingdom?

_____

_____

_____

_____

Why do you believe Jesus spoke so strongly in regard to the marriage relationship?

_____

_____

_____

_____

What do you believe to be the single most important factor in a marriage that truly models the relationship between Christ and His church?

_____

_____

_____

Kingdom Life—*The Honor of Submission*

Priscilla was obviously a woman of courage, conviction, and faith. And we have seen time and again that these qualities are only developed by time spent in the presence of God. Priscilla was spiritually strong and not thrown by times of difficulty in her life.

This godly woman seemed to understand the godly principles of headship and submission. She must have realized the trust God placed in His women when He called on them to submit to their husbands. It is a principle of the kingdom that "if anyone desires to be first, he shall be last of all and servant of all" (Mark 9:35). By calling on His women to voluntarily submit to their husbands, He placed them in the place of greatest blessing, for the first shall be last and the last first.

Turn to Ephesians 5:22–33. Notice how these verses put such demands upon the Christian husband that it is impossible to see how a charge of male chauvinism could justly be made against the Bible, or how a license to exploit wives could ever be claimed. But the Bible also has its requirements of a wife: she is to acknowledge her husband's calling as head of the family, respond to his leadership, listen to him, praise him, be unified in purpose and will with him, and be a true helper. No wife can do this by mere willpower or resolve, but since you are "His workmanship" (Ephesians 2:8–10), God will help bring this about.

It takes great spiritual fortitude to stand in faith and support a husband during times of trial or difficulty. But the woman who has clothed her spirit with the scarlet blood of the Lamb (Proverbs 31:21) will be ready both "in season and out of season" (2 Timothy 4:2).

No husband is without failure or weakness simply because he is a fallen human being. The danger is in allowing the devil to prey on your natural inclinations to exaggerate your mate's failures and inadequacies, sow suspicion and jealousy, indulge your self-pity, or insist that you deserve something better. He will attempt to convince you to act in a manner that would be other than pleasing to God. Decide *today* that you will be a wife who does her husband good; and ask of the Lord whatever you need to enable you to live that out.

Read Ephesians 5:24; 1 Peter 3:1–6.

Questions:

What does the Bible give as a model for a wife in showing respect (reverence) to her husband? (Ephesians 5:24)

✎ _____

_____

_____

In light of what has just been studied, does respect have to be earned, or should it be given voluntarily? Why?

✎ _____

_____

_____

With the preceding sessions in mind, what is your current understanding of submission?

✎ _____

_____

_____

How can submission become a means to greater power and freedom in ministry? Support your answer biblically.

✎ _____

_____

_____

Record Your Thoughts

Very few of us will have the opportunity to share the gospel of Jesus Christ before large groups; not many of us will lead a home church or be in a position of highly influential, widespread ministry. But we can all impact people for the sake of His kingdom. There are many organizations devoted to helping those in need, and most are desperate for volunteers. Check with your church or other local agencies for referrals of places where you can serve. The need may even be as close as next door. What better way to show a neighbor the love of God and the relevancy of the gospel to their world than by serving them as Christ taught us to. Take a moment and write down some practical ways that you will reach out to others this month in the name of the Lord.

Also, take some time to read through Proverbs 31:10–31 once again. List as many qualities of godly virtue as you can find that are either given directly ("does him good") or implied (is thrifty). Try to find at least twenty. Keep this list and choose one per week to either refresh yourself on or to newly incorporate into your life. You can do all things through Christ who strengthens you!

SESSION TWELVE

Lydia, Daughter of Hospitality

 Kingdom Key—*Golden Rule*

Matthew 7:12 Therefore, whatever you want men to do to you, do also to them, for this is the Law and the Prophets.

This verse is the famous "Golden Rule." Its truth is so profound, it is known in just about every culture. Its full expression is found in Leviticus 19:18. In both instances, we are called to love others in real and practical ways. Love, as used in Leviticus 19:18, could be understood as esteem—respect, value, or regard. Love of others begins with self-esteem, for those who live with the painful inner turmoil of self-recrimination are not free to look outward beyond their pain. We are to love others *as* we love ourselves. The importance of holding others in esteem, desiring their good at all times, is summarized by Paul when he writes, "But the greatest of these [virtues] is love" (1 Corinthians 13:13).

All nonbiblical literary efforts to define love fall silent before apostle Paul's magnificent hymn of love. It is a description of Christ and the love He enables when He comes to indwell us. The miracle of Christ's indwelling power is that the love He revealed is exactly the love He will communicate to others through us. When this quality of love is the basis of a relationship, the miracle of unity is possible.

Read 1 Corinthians 13:1–13.

Questions:

What heart attitude do you believe lies at the core of the qualities of love listed in this passage?

_____

_____

_____

In what way does personal choice impact the ability to live out these qualities in relationship?

_____

_____

_____

What do you believe lies at the heart of hospitality as a function in the body of Christ?

_____

_____

_____

How might living out the qualities of love enable you to practice hospitality more easily?

_____

_____

_____

In your current view, what is the relationship between hospitality and leadership in the body of Christ?

_____

_____

_____

Word Wealth—*Hospitality*

Hospitality, *philoxenos* (fil-ox'-en-os); Strong's #5382: To entertain strangers, be fond of guests, given to (lover of) hospitality. This Greek word is a combination of two Greek words: *philos*, meaning a friend or neighbor (or as an adjective, fondly or friendly); and *xenos*, which means guest or stranger. Hospitality, then, should reach beyond those we know to encompass all—strangers as well as friends.

Kingdom Life—*Ambassadors of Christ*

Lydia was among a small group of people in Philippi who met along the riverside for prayer. Since Jewish law required the establishment of a synagogue when there was a population of at least ten men in a community, the absence of a synagogue in Philippi indicates a small Jewish population. This little band was later converted to Christianity and grew into the church to whom Paul wrote his letter to the Philippians. They became a body with a strong missionary zeal and a lively spirit of fellowship, and they encouraged and supported Paul's ministry.

Paul wrote to the church at Philippi to encourage them in their faith. In this letter, he speaks often of joy. Paul contends that true joy is not a surface emotion that depends on favorable circumstances of the moment. Christian joy is independent of outward conditions. It ultimately arises from fellowship with the risen, glorified Christ.

Paul further describes a joy that springs from fellowship—the loving relationship between believers. Godly relationships are a powerful tool; they encourage and promote spiritual growth, but they also act as a beacon to the world—showing forth the love of Christ. The love of God in action through the lives of believers is like a light in the darkness that leads others safely into the kingdom.

Read John 13:35; Philippians 2:1–4; Colossians 3:17; 1 Thessalonians 3:12.

Questions:

What aspects of 1 Corinthians 13:1–13 are employed when one practices hospitality?

✎_____

_____

_____

How might a spirit of hospitality be used of God to bring others into the kingdom?

✎_____

_____

_____

_____

What are some other benefits that could be found in practicing hospitality?

✎_____

_____

_____

Do you find hospitality difficult or does it come naturally to you? Why do you believe this is so?

✎_____

_____

_____

In light of what has been presented thus far in this session, who do you believe is called to practice hospitality?

✎_____

_____

Kingdom Life—*All One Family*

Leviticus 19:34 contains timeless words that clearly establish God's guidelines on how to interact with strangers (or those not of your own household). The spirit of these guidelines recurs throughout both the OT and NT. God indicates that He expects us to relate to strangers in deep, unselfish, servant-spirited, Christian love. He reminds His people that they, who once were foreigners in the land of Egypt, should above all others remember how it feels to be treated as outsiders. In this verse, we are given two lessons: 1) we all have experienced rejection. We need to remember how it feels and never manifest it toward others. God's further instructions on the treatment of strangers are opposite to normal, worldly standards. The Lord says that when strangers come into our homes, they are to be treated as "one born among you," that is, as blood relatives! Since the Jews placed great emphasis upon bloodlines and lineage, God's use of this terminology had an extremely high impact, underscoring the significance of strangers in God's eyes; 2) all of humanity is one family. Treat others that way.

Read Luke 14:13, 14; Romans 12:9–13; Hebrews 13:2; 1 John 3:16, 17.

Questions:

What do you see as some other reasons God places such a high value on hospitality?

To invite someone into your home is to show them honor. What impact could this have on reaching others for Christ? What impact could this have on a brother or sister in the Lord?

Why do you believe it is important for those in leadership of the body of Christ to practice hospitality?

✎ _____

_____

_____

What is your reaction to Hebrews 13:2? Why do you think angels visit without revealing their identity?

✎ _____

_____

_____

Probing the Depths

Hospitality is the practice of entertaining strangers graciously. Hospitality was considered important in Bible times. In the Old Testament, Abraham was the host to angels unaware; he invited strangers into his house, washed their feet, prepared fresh meat, had Sarah bake bread, and later accompanied them as they left (Genesis 18:1–15). Even today, a traditional greeting to the guests among the Bedouin people of the Middle East is "You are among your family."

Hospitality was specifically commanded by God (Leviticus 19:33, 34; Luke 14:13, 14; Romans 12:13). It was to be characteristic of all believers (1 Peter 4:9), especially bishops (Titus 1:7–8; 1 Timothy 3:2). Jesus emphasized the importance of hospitality by answering the question of who should inherit the kingdom: "I was a stranger and you took Me in" (Matthew 25:35).

Several Old Testament personalities set a good example for all believers in the practice of hospitality. These included Abraham (Genesis 18:1–8); David (2 Samuel 6:19); the Shunammite woman (2 Kings 4:8–10); Nehemiah (Nehemiah 5:17, 18); and Job (Job 31:17–20).

Psalm 23 concludes with a portrait of a host who prepares a table for the weary, anoints the head of the guest with oil, and shows every kindness so that the guest's cup runs over. The psalmist sees the Lord Himself as Host; His hospitality exceeds all others.

The New Testament also gives examples of gracious hospitality: Mary (Matthew 26:6–13); Martha (Luke 10:38); the early Christians (Acts 2:45, 46); Lydia (Acts 16:14, 15); and Priscilla and Aquila (Acts 18:26). The Greek word translated as hospitality in the New Testament literally means "love of strangers."

Kingdom Life—*All Means All*

Review the Word Wealth entry on hospitality. Included in the meanings are "lover of hospitality" and "fond of guests." Hence, there *are* those who are specifically gifted to host others. But just as intercessors being anointed for prayer doesn't exclude the rest of us from praying, neither is hospitality to be left for those to whom it comes more naturally.

Let's read a few passages and consider their meaning to us:

- Turn to both 1 Timothy 3:2 and Titus 1:7, 8. What specific groups were required to be hospitable?

_____

_____

_____

_____

- Now turn to Romans 12:9–21. Paul exhorted *all* believers to show true Christian love through a number of duties. Which of these are mentioned in verses 13 and 20? (Notice "given to" is also translated "pursuing.")

_____

_____

_____

- Turn now to 1 Peter 4:8–11, where believers are asked to show "fervent love for one another." What is included as one expression of that fervency? (v. 9)

_____

_____

_____

- According to 1 Timothy 5:10, what are listed as the "good works" of a widow?

_____

_____

_____

- In summary, record who is to be given to hospitality and who is exempt.

_____

_____

_____

It is clear that hospitality is a form of ministry in which God desires every believer to participate. It is evident from what we've already studied that believers should show hospitality to one another. This priority is most clearly seen in the fact that the early church actually began by people opening their homes (Acts 2:46; 20:20; 1 Corinthians 16:19). But we must not limit our expression of hospitality to those we know. We must reach out to those who need us and open our homes to them as readily as we are called to open our hearts to their need.

Kingdom Life—*Serve with Grace*

Hospitality does not require extravagance or abundance. Sometimes, the simplest of expressions (for example, a cup of coffee, or a soft drink), when done with the love and compassion of Christ, are far more meaningful to someone than a huge display. In the case of biblical hospitality, it is truly the thought that counts.

There is one woman in Scripture who may have done well to realize true hospitality is more a matter of heart than action. Turn to Luke 10:38–42 to read about Martha.

Martha and Mary were sisters who lived in the village of Bethany, a suburb of Jerusalem. It appears Martha was the elder, for verse 38 speaks of Martha's receiving Jesus "into her house." Thus, it is likely Martha felt more keenly the domestic responsibilities of keeping house and the demands of providing hospitality.

Martha was caring for the needs of her guests, but her busyness distracted her and most likely proved a distraction for her guests. (A stressed-out host can't put guests at ease.) Obviously, Martha was allowing herself to become far too preoccupied with the details of serving her guests and was perhaps feeling pressured that everything was not "just so." In verse 42, Jesus so lovingly reminds her of what is actually valuable and worthwhile: *the giving and receiving of ministry.* That is also the guiding principle behind biblical hospitality. It is doubtful whether people will remember what they ate, or how it was served, months after leaving your home. But they will always remember what they came away with in their hearts.

Hospitality is a joyous way to extend the life of Christ to others in the comfort and intimacy of your own home. It can be a stretch in many ways, for it is not always convenient, it may not go as you planned, and you may be required to receive those who are in a rather unlovable condition, whether spiritually, emotionally, or physically. But consider our model, the Lord Jesus Christ, who so lovingly and willingly, with humble graciousness, reached toward us in spite of our unworthiness, and extended to us the hope of eternal life.

Read Matthew 25:31–46.

Questions:

What difference might recalling Jesus' words in this passage make in practicing hospitality?

✎ _____

_____

_____

How is practicing hospitality another way of living out the Golden Rule?

✎ _____

_____

_____

Besides your home, name other places wherein you may practice godly hospitality.

✎ _____

_____

_____

What practical steps can you take to improve your ability to be hospitable?

✎ _____

_____

_____

Record Your Thoughts

As you seek to live out the joy of being a daughter of Almighty God, remember the words of Joel: "And it shall come to pass in the last days, says God, that I will pour out of My Spirit on all flesh; your sons and your daughters shall prophesy, your young men shall see visions, your old men shall dream dreams. And on My menservants and on My maidservants I will pour out My Spirit in those days; and they shall prophesy" (Acts 2:17, 18). Every believer is anointed to be a priest and a king in the kingdom of God (Revelation 1:6; 5:10).

What has most impacted you in this study? How will this new insight enable you to step out into the destiny God has prepared for you?

✎ _____

_____

_____

Go back through each of the lessons and make note of your strengths and weaknesses in light of what you have studied in this guide. Next to each strength, note at least one way in which you can put this ability to use as a handmaiden of the Lord. For each weakness, find a passage of Scripture that speaks to God's provision in that area. Then determine a course of action to improve your ability in the weaker aspects of your nature.

✎ _____

_____

_____

You are a beloved daughter of Almighty God. He created you with a purpose and He has a specific plan for your life. He will lead you and guide you and teach you all you need to minister effectively in His name—to one or to thousands. Remember, when He calls, He enables; you can trust Him to give you all you need to do all He asks.

ADDITIONAL OBSERVATIONS

ABOUT THE AUTHORS

About the Executive Editor

JACK W. HAYFORD, noted pastor, teacher, writer, and composer, is the Executive Editor of the complete series, working with the publisher in the conceiving and developing of each of the books.

Dr. Hayford served as senior pastor of The Church on the Way, the First Foursquare Church of Van Nuys, California for 31 years, from 1969 to 2000. He founded The King's University—Los Angeles, where he serves as chancellor, while continuing his ministry to pastors and leaders globally. He and his wife, Anna, have four married children, all of whom are committed to Christ and are active in either pastoral ministry or a local church. As General Editor of the Spirit-Filled Life Bible, Pastor Hayford led a four-year project, which has resulted in the availability of one of today's most practical and popular study Bibles. He is author of more than 52 books, including *A Passion for Fullness*, *The Beauty of Spiritual Language*, *Rebuilding the Real You*, *Prayer Is Invading the Impossible*, and *Penetrating the Darkness*. His musical compositions number over 600 songs, including the widely sung "Majesty."

About the Writer

M. WENDY PARRISH, and her husband Frank, colead World MAP, providing ministry training for millions of underserved church leaders in more than 140 developing nations.

Frank and Wendy have been married since 1981 and have two grown sons and a third son who is with the Lord. In addition to serving with Frank in pastoral ministry, Wendy has been a homemaker, magazine editor, speaker, worship leader, communications director at a megachurch, and published author.

Wendy attended LIFE Pacific College but says her real training for ministry was the eight years she spent homeschooling her three sons. Wendy's broad range of home and workplace experiences gives her a unique understanding of, and compassion for, the challenges faced by today's Christian woman.